FINLAND

Tan Chung Lee

Marshall Cavendish
Benchmark

New York

PICTURE CREDITS
Cover photo: © David Bartruff / Danita Delimont.com
age fotostock / GONZALO AZUMENDI: 111 • age fotostock / NILS-JOHAN NORENLIND: 38, 85 • age fotostock / SYLVAIN GRANDADAM: 5, 59, 77, 84, 88, 116, 122 • alt.TYPE / Reuters: 31, 32, 36, 39, 110, 112, 121 • Bes Stock: 19 • Camera Press: 25, 97, 127 • David Simson: 20, 44, 60, 69, 81, 83 • Finnish Embassy: 3, 96, 113 • Finnish Tourist Board: 12, 107 • Focus Team: 6, 10, 11, 16, 46, 48, 49, 51, 61, 62, 76, 78, 124, 128, 129 • HBL Network Photo Agency: 4, 114 • Hutchison: 73, 105, 123 • Image Bank: 45 • International Photobank: 1, 28, 55, 66, 93 • Life File: 7, 13, 14, 20, 33, 34, 41, 43, 52, 58, 67, 72, 75, 86, 91, 115, 119, 126 • Lonely Planet Images: 9, 56, 79, 80, 87, 89, 92, 104, 108 • National Museum of Finland: 17, 22, 24, 102, 109, 120 • Photobank Singapore: 21, 65, 70, 117 • Pressfoto: 15, 27, 63, 68, 71, 74, 82, 94, 95, 98, 99, 100, 101, 106, 118, 125 • STOCKFOOD: 131 • STOCKFOOD / STUDIO DHS: 130 • SUPERSTOCK: 64

PRECEDING PAGE
Helsinki's Senate Square with the Lutheran Cathedral and statue of Alexander II.

Editorial Director (U.S.): Michelle Bisson
Editors: Deborah Grahame, Mabelle Yeo, Ruth Wan
Copyreaders: Deborah Federhen, Daphne Hougham
Designer: Jailani Basari
Cover picture researcher: Connie Gardner
Picture researchers: Thomas Khoo, Joshua Ang

Marshall Cavendish Benchmark
99 White Plains Road
Tarrytown, NY 10591
Web site: www.marshallcavendish.us

Originated and designed by Times Editions
An imprint of Marshall Cavendish International (Asia) Private Limited
A member of Times Publishing Limited

Library of Congress Cataloging-in-Publication Data
Tan, Chung Lee, 1949–
    Finland / [Tan Chung Lee]. — 2nd.
      p. cm. — (Cultures of the world)
    Summary: "Provides comprehensive information on the geography, history, wildlife, governmental structure, economy, cultural diversity, peoples, religion, and culture of Finland" — Provided by publisher.
    Includes bibliographical references and index.
      ISBN-13: 978-0-7614-2073-6
      ISBN-10: 0-7614-2073-8
    1. Finland—Juvenile literature. I. Title.

DL1012.T35 2007
  948.97—dc22   2006015897

Printed in China

9 8 7 6 5 4 3 2

CONTENTS

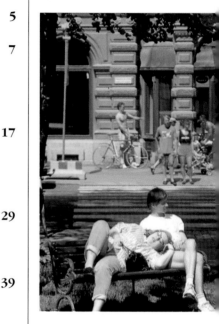

Finns enjoying a summer afternoon in a park.

A Finnish boy in traditional Sami costume feeding
a reindeer in Lapland.

INTRODUCTION

TRADITIONALLY, FINLAND HAS BEEN pictured as a land of incredible beauty—an idyllic land with endless stretches of forest, thousands of lakes, and shores dotted with log cabins that are the summer homes of many Finnish families.

One of the world's most popular cell phone companies, Nokia, is Finnish. When Nokia pioneered the first cell phones, Finland suddenly gained a reputation as a modern and high-tech nation, especially in information and communications technology.

This reputation may have been new, but it is rooted in deep traditions. The Finns have always had the aptitude and capability for novelty. Theirs is a psyche shaped by history and geography. Centuries of political domination by Sweden and Russia and long, harsh winters have imbued in the Finns a survival instinct and a spirit of innovation and adaptability.

From being known as an isolated country tucked in the northerly regions to becoming an inventive nation, Finland is today one of the leaders of the world's technological revolution.

GEOGRAPHY

FINLAND IS THE WORLD'S MOST NORTHERLY country, with one-quarter of its total land area of 130,558 square miles (338,144 square km) lying north of the Arctic Circle. Although it is the seventh-largest country in Europe in terms of area (about the size of New England, New York, and New Jersey combined) it is also one of the least populous, with 5.3 million people.

The country stretches 720 miles (1,160 km) from north to south, and 335 miles (540 km) from east to west. Except for a 680-mile-long (1,100-km) coastline, the rest of Finland's 2,240-mile (3,600-km) frontier is shared with other countries: Sweden to the west, Norway to the north, and Russia to the east.

Much of Finland comprises low-lying plain. About 70 percent of the land area is forested, only 8 percent is cultivated land, and the rest is made up of swamps, arctic fells, and sand.

Finland is a land of thousands of lakes and islands, as well as acres of untouched forests. It has sunlit "nightless" summers, snow-covered winters, and brilliantly-colored landscapes in the fall.

Left: **Snow covers a lake in Vaasa. Sometimes the temperature drops so low that the entire Gulf of Bothnia freezes.**

Opposite: **A view of the Lake District from within the lush forest along its banks.**

Opposite: **View of the snow-covered forest and hilly landscape of Valtavaara Ridge in Oulu Province's Kuusamo City.**

TOPOGRAPHY AND LANDSCAPE

The bedrock beneath Finland is among the world's oldest. Much of the country's physical features were formed during the last Ice Age, which began 40 million years ago and ended 10,000 years ago when the continental glaciers receded. The power of the moving ice sheets carved out the lake basins that lie in a northwest to southeast direction, and where they stopped, they left behind a rim of geologic debris that formed the Salpausselkä Ridge, which is south of the Lake District, while water from the melting glaciers filled the lakes. The swift-running currents of the melting glacier formed several ridges, known as eskers, which run parallel to the lake basins. The lake-encircled ridges near the city of Savonlinna in Finland's Lake District are a prime example.

Since the disappearance of the continental glaciers, the country's land mass has been rising from the sea in a process known as isostatic uplift—as the continental glaciers shift, they have the effect of depressing the land over which they travel; but when the weight of the ice is lifted after the glaciers move on, the land rises. Even though it has been 10,000 years since the last ice sheets have receded, Finland is still recovering from this immense load. The land along the Gulf of Finland, for example, rises 12 inches (30 cm) every 100 years, while on the Gulf of Bothnia, it goes up by as much as 36 inches (90 cm) during the same period. It is estimated that Finland's total land mass increases by 2.7 square miles (7 square km) each year. Most of the land along the coast comprises low-lying plains. Inland, there are mounds and hills interspersed with lakes and rivers.

Finland is such a long country that the landscape from south to north varies greatly; the gently-rolling rural landscape in the south gradually gives way to hills and vast forested areas in the north. The only mountainous area in the country is in the northwest, near Norway, in an area known as Upland Finland, where peaks average 3,300 feet (1,000 m). The exception is Haltiatunturi, which at 4,343 feet (1,324 m), is Finland's highest point.

More than two-thirds of Finland is covered with forest. Finland has more forest area per capita than any other country in Europe with approximately 9.8 acres (4 ha) of forest per person. Wild animals such as elk, bears, and, occasionally, wolves roam the forests of spruce, birch, and pine. In the foothills of Lapland—a region above the Arctic Circle comprising not only a part of Finland but also parts of Sweden, Norway, and Russia—reindeer herds wander freely.

COAST AND ARCHIPELAGO

Southwest Finland, located along the coast, is one of the country's most beautiful areas and its most historical. The main centers are Helsinki, the capital, and Turku, the former capital, noted for its medieval castle and cathedral. In the west, the Gulf of Bothnia, an arm of the Baltic Sea, forms a natural barrier between Sweden and Finland; to the south, the Gulf of Finland separates the country from the Baltic states of Estonia, Latvia, and Lithuania.

A look at a map of Finland shows an archipelago of 17,000 tree-covered islands and smaller skerries (small, rocky islands, or reefs) scattered off its coast, extending right up to the Åland Islands. The waters around this scenic archipelago are a yachtsman's paradise.

In the Lake District, many of the lakes are connected by short rivers and channels, making it easier for people to get around by boat.

THE LAKE DISTRICT

Finland has more lakes than any other country—about 188,000 lakes that provide 121 feet (37 m) of lakefront per person. Twenty-two of its lakes measure over 75 square miles (200 square km) in size. The biggest lake in Finland is Lake Saimaa at 443 square miles (1,147 square km) which, with other lakes, forms the Saimaa Lake System, comprising a whopping 1,850 square miles (4,790 square km).

The beautiful lakelands are at the heart of Finland, occupying almost a third of the whole country. Thousands of lakes flow down the many rivers to drain into the Baltic Sea. Before the days of roads and railways, the lakes formed narrow waterways linking towns across central Finland. Ships were the only means of travel then. Today, one can travel through central Finland by road, in addition to the more traditional route in a passenger ship.

LAPLAND—LAND OF THE MIDNIGHT SUN

Covering the extreme north of Finland and located almost entirely above the Arctic Circle, Lapland is the land of the midnight sun. From mid-May, for 70 days and nights, the sun never dips below the horizon, even at midnight. This is followed by a 50-day "sunset" when the sky gets progressively darker, culminating in the sunless days of *kaamos* (KAAH-mos), when it is nighttime even at noon—a phenomenon that lasts nearly six months. This is the season of the spectacular Aurora Borealis, also known as Northern Lights, which dance across the arctic sky, setting it ablaze with shafts of colored light.

Many people visit Lapland to experience the midnight sun or *kaamos*. In addition, Lapland's great wilderness is a big attraction. Lapland, which occupies one-third of the land area of Finland, has plenty of open space and herds of roaming reindeer. Unlike the rest of Finland, there are few lakes in Lapland, but there are many rivers separated by vast stretches of uninhabited land. Lots of pine and spruce can be found in the valleys. Above the valleys are fells, which are gently-rounded hills that are the result of the erosion by glaciers. The fells are treeless except for occasional scrub.

HELSINKI

Helsinki became the capital of Finland in 1812, replacing Turku. It has a unique character as it bears the stamp of both its Swedish and Russian heritages. Founded in 1550, Helsinki was known in Swedish as Helsingfors. In 1748 the Swedes

built a castle on the island of Suomenlinna, just outside the city. Yet there is also much about Helsinki that reminds the visitor of the time when Finland was governed by Russia as a Grand Duchy, particularly the magnificent Senate Square, with its Lutheran Cathedral and surrounding neoclassical buildings, designed by Carl Ludwig Engel from 1818 to 1822 to commemorate Finland's integration into the Russian empire. The Uspenski Orthodox Cathedral, with its gilded onion domes, and the city's

At the height of summer, the sun can be seen even at night, giving the phenomenon the appropriate name of "midnight sun."

many Russian restaurants add to Helsinki's czarist flavor. Architecturally Helsinki bears such a great resemblance to czarist Saint Petersburg that several U.S. movies with Russian settings have been shot on location in Helsinki instead of Russia.

The city is also known for its Art Nouveau buildings which were built in the 1900s. The best example of Art Nouveau is the striking Helsinki Central Railway Station, the work of Eliel Saarinen. The presence of many parks and Helsinki's location on the coastline of the Baltic Sea make for an attractive and scenic setting. With a population of only 560,000, the city is not congested and has many open spaces.

TAMPERE

Tampere, Finland's second largest city with a population of about 200,000, enjoys a beautiful setting between the lakes of Näsijärvi and Pyhäjärvi in southwest Finland. In the past, it was a manufacturing center, as its location on the water's edge made it the perfect area for industries. Today, many of the factories have been renovated for use as cultural centers and Tampere has gained a reputation as a leisure and cultural city. It hosts the Tampere Film Festival every March and Tammerfest, a youth rock festival, every July. The Tampere Biennale of new Finnish music was held in April 2006 for the 11th time.

TURKU

Turku is Finland's main port and its oldest—and third-largest—city, with 175,000 inhabitants. It has the country's largest Swedish-speaking population. It was a thriving trading center as early as the 13th century and served as the capital of Finland until 1812. The city offers many historical sights. The famous medieval Turku Castle is the main attraction. Now used as a museum, it was Sweden's major defensive position in Finland during the Middle Ages and survived several battles and sieges.

Another medieval attraction, Turku Cathedral, took two centuries to complete after construction started in the 13th century. Many well-known figures in Finnish history are buried in the main cathedral and its side chapels. The scenic beauty can be best appreciated by taking a cruise and sailing among its many islands.

CLIMATE

Despite its northerly location, Finland has a milder climate than expected, thanks to the Baltic Sea, the inland waters, and the westerly winds from

Even though Tampere is an important inland urban center with many cultural attractions, nature is never far away. There are about 180 lakes within the city's borders.

the Atlantic, which are warmed by the Gulf Stream. The country enjoys an annual average temperature that is 43°F (6°C) warmer than other countries on the same latitude. However, east and southeast winds from the Eurasian continent bring heat waves in summer and cold spells in winter.

There are regional differences in the climate as well as variations in the seasons. Winter is a long season in the north, with snow arriving as early as October and lasting until late April in Lapland. In the south, the first snow appears in December and the days are short, lasting under six hours. The average winter temperature in the south is 26°F (-3°C).

Summers in Finland are warm. In the south, the temperature in July averages 68°F (20°C), although it can go up to 86°F (30°C) during the day. The south also receives 8 inches (20 cm) more rain than in the north; on the average, the country has about 100 days of rain each year.

During the winter, birds depend on their feathers to protect them from the extreme cold, and their resting spots are carefully chosen not only to provide shelter, but also to catch whatever warmth the sun may provide.

FLORA AND FAUNA

Finland lies in the northern coniferous forest zone and its flora and fauna are typical of this zone. The most common vegetation is forest consisting of mainly birch, pine, and spruce. Oak is found in the extreme south and southwest. The country also has substantial areas of swampland.

There are at least 60 different species of mammals. Common animals include the wolf, European brown bear, lynx, wolverine, and Saimaa seals, while moose, reindeer, beavers, and Finnish deer are also abundant. Some animals, such as moose, are so numerous that hunting is allowed to keep them in check. Foxes, squirrels, and hare are plentiful in the forests.

There are more than 350 bird species in Finland, and most of them are migratory. Native bird species include the blackbird, white-tailed eagle, osprey, eagle, and whooping swan, which is Finland's national bird. The white-tailed eagle was once considered an endangered species, but it is now increasing in number.

Fish is plentiful and over 70 species can be found in Finland. The commercially-important ones are the Baltic herring and whitefish. Reptiles and frogs are less common, with 11 species found. The most common snake is the European adder or common viper.

The brown bear is Finland's national animal. There are about 1,000 bears left in the country today, and bear hunting is strictly regulated. Finland has a good record for animal conservation.

HISTORY

FINLAND DATES ITS HISTORY from the end of the last Ice Age 40,000 years ago. The country's first settlers who moved into the area of forests and lakes between the Gulf of Finland, the Gulf of Bothnia, and Lake Ladoga were said to belong to the Finno-Ugrian group of people. It was only much later that they were joined by the Finns—the settlers who gave Finland its name—who migrated from the southern parts of the Gulf of Finland. Subsequently, about 2,000 years ago, migrants from the Baltic areas added to the demographic mix.

There are indications that the upper part of Finland above the Arctic Circle was occupied during the Stone Age (7500–1500 B.C.), mainly along the coast. Later, during the Bronze Age (1500–500 B.C.) and Iron Age (500 B.C.–A.D. 400), the settlers moved inland, developing trade and cultural ties with regions east and west of them. During the Viking period, close links with Scandinavia and Russia were forged. The Vikings raided far and wide, working eastward as far as Constantinople, which is present-day Istanbul. Their route took them through the Lake Mälaren valley and the Götaland region in Sweden, and southward across the Gulf of Finland.

Records indicate that Viking expeditions started from around A.D. 800. Their campaigns into Russia and Byzantium continued well into the 10th and 11th centuries and were said to have also involved the participation of some Finns. When the Western Scandinavians converted to Christianity and ended their marauding on distant territories, the Finnish and Baltic pagans continued their exploits, which are recounted in the epic *Kalevala* tales.

Above: **This Stone Age mace in the shape of an elk's head was found in Finland.**

Opposite: **Statue of Alexander II in Helsinki's Senate Square.**

The Swedish period lasted from 1200 to 1809.

THE SWEDISH PERIOD

Finland was rather fragmented until about the 13th century. Three main tribes—the Finns, the Tavastians, and the Karelians—dominated different

In 1323 a border was established between Sweden and Novgorod, resulting in the division of Karelia and its people between two kingdoms, religions, and cultures. Eastern Karelia came under Novgorod, linking it to Russia and the Orthodox Church. West of the border was western Karelia and southern Finland, which came under the Swedish kingdom and the Catholic Church. In 1362 Finland was given the right to participate in electing the Swedish king through a legislative body that was the foundation of today's Eduskuntar *(parliament).*

areas and were hostile toward one another. The Finns in the southwest and in Häme had links with their neighbors west of their border, the Tavastians lived inland in southern Finland, and the Karelians were oriented toward their eastern neighbors. In addition, part of western Finland, the archipelago, and the Åland Islands had once been part of the Central Swedish military and economic system.

Sweden, under the influence of the Roman Catholic Church and the Russian city of Novgorod at that time, sought to gain political control over this fractious country. It began its encroachment upon Finland in the 12th century. The first crusade in 1155, led by King Eric and Saint Henry, the Bishop of Uppsala, was launched to increase Swedish influence. Missionaries conducted their work around Turku and the inner areas around Tampere. Christianity was firmly established in southwest Finland in the mid-12th century. After the Pope gave his sanction in 1216, the Swedes continued their quest with a second crusade into Tavastia. They entered Häme, Uusimaa, and Karelia, where they built a castle. Soon, Swedish immigrants moved in to settle along the coast. In the meantime, Novgorod was trying to extend its influence along the Gulf of Finland and the area around Lake Ladoga, while Denmark and Germany were gaining control of the coastal regions along the eastern route.

Sweden and Novgorod continued their battle for the control of Finland and the eastern coast of the Gulf of Finland in 1293, when Sweden built the Wiborg fortress and city. In 1300 they established a fort on the banks of the River Neva but this was destroyed by Novgorod.

The war finally ended in 1323 with the Treaty of Pähkinäsaari, which established a border between Sweden and Novgorod for the first time. The eastern part of Karelia was made part of Novgorod, linking it to Russia and the Orthodox Church. All areas west of the border, including western Karelia and southern Finland, came under the Swedish kingdom and the Roman Catholic Church. The new border thus divided the people of Karelia between two kingdoms, religions, and cultures.

Under the rule of Sweden, Swedish law and the Scandinavian social system were established. The Finns enjoyed full political rights. In 1362 they were given the right to participate in the elections of the king through the Finnish body of *lagmän* (LAG-men), now known as *Eduskuntar* (EH-dus-koon-tah). In the 16th century, a legislative assembly representing four groups—the nobility, clergy, burghers, and farmers—was set up, known as the Diet of the Four Estates.

THE GREAT POWER PERIOD

Sweden's Great Power period (1617–1721) began with the reign of Gustavus II Adolphus and his expansionist policy targeting the Baltic countries, Poland, and Germany. As the Baltic region gradually came under Swedish control, the border of Finland was pushed farther east. The Finns were conscripted into battle for the Swedes.

Another significant development during this period was the process of "Swedification" in Finland. There was a tightening of administrative control in all aspects of Finnish life to ensure uniformity with Stockholm, Sweden's capital city and its administrative, economic, and cultural hub. The highest posts were filled by Swedes and the Swedish language grew in importance in Finland.

Saint Olaf's Castle at Olavinlinna was constructed in the 15th century. The castle has three brick towers and served as both a Swedish and Russian fortress.

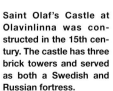

A war memorial in Hanko stands as a lonely reminder of the struggle with Russia for control of Finland. Finland's importance to Russia lay in its strategic location near Saint Petersburg, Russia's western capital. By controlling the Gulf of Finland, Russia could prevent enemy attacks.

RUSSIAN OCCUPATION

Russia, in the meantime, began to expand westward, encroaching upon Finland and other Swedish-occupied territories. From 1710 to 1714 Russia took over the whole of Finland, as far as the Åland Islands. The occupation period, known as the Great Wrath, ended in 1721 with the Treaty of Uusikaupunki (also known as the Treaty of Nystad). Although Sweden regained control of Finland, it lost Karelia to the Russians. Another war, known as the War of the Hats, broke out between 1741 and 1743. Russia occupied Finland yet again during a period known as the Lesser Wrath. Under the Peace of Turku in 1743, Russia agreed to withdraw its troops in return for more territory, pushing the border farther westward. Sweden ceded the fortified towns of Hamina and Lappeenranta in southeast Finland and the Olavinlinna fortress to Russia.

There were feelings in some quarters that Finland should separate from Sweden. Finnish representatives in the Diet at Stockholm demanded special aid to compensate for what their country had suffered during the periods of Russian occupation. This resulted in the introduction of economic reforms and a boosting of Finnish defense over the next few decades. Trade restrictions were removed, a fortress on Suomenlinna was built, and a strong coastal naval fleet was developed. Living standards improved, especially during the reign of Gustavus III (1771–92), and new towns were established. Finnish literature developed. The Finnish language was accepted in the Diet and for use on currency, and more Finns were appointed to the civil service.

From 1788 to 1790 there was another war with Russia. An attempt among some military officers to separate Finland from Sweden found little support. However, this secessionist attempt was to influence Russia's actions in a war from 1808 to 1809 when, instead of returning occupied territory to Sweden, the Russians held on to Finland, making it a buffer zone with its own Diet and administration.

FINLAND AS AN AUTONOMOUS GRAND DUCHY

The czar of Russia, Alexander I, personally supervised the affairs of Finland. The Finns had already pledged their loyalty to the czar in a session of the Finnish Diet held in the city of Porvoo in 1809. In return for their allegiance, the czar promised that he would let them continue practicing the Evangelical Lutheran faith, and that they would have equal constitutional laws and rights. In effect, Finland became an autonomous Grand Duchy with its own institutions—a sort of separate state within Russia. The czar was the constitutional monarch and was represented by a governor-general. The highest government body was the Senate, made up of Finns who still maintained their Diet of the Four Estates. The Finns also had their own representative at the court of Saint Petersburg, who could personally present matters concerning Finland to the czar.

Uspenski Cathedral in Helsinki shows the Russian influence on Finnish culture.

Tsar Alexander I, Grand Duke of Finland, addressing the Finnish Assembly at the opening ceremony of the Diet in Porvoo in 1809, held at the city's cathedral. The oil painting by Emanuel Thelning was completed between 1809 and 1812.

To weaken the influence of Sweden, the czar encouraged building and development in Finland, and Helsinki was made the new capital. The system of roads and canals was improved. Elegant buildings went up to beautify the city.

The period of autonomy gave rise to a new Finnish national consciousness. Finnish literature developed and there was a movement to promote Finnish as an official language alongside Swedish. During the reigns of Alexander III (1881–94) and Nicholas II (1894–1917), questions were raised about Finland's autonomous status by the extremist Pan-Slavist group in Russia. The Finns were no longer divided among themselves by language, but by their outlook on Russia.

The Russo-Japanese War (1904–05), in which Russia was defeated, resulted in unrest that extended to Finland, forcing the czar to liberalize his rule. This led to radical parliamentary reform in Finland in 1906, with a new single-chamber parliament replacing the Diet of the Four Estates. Universal suffrage was introduced, and the right to vote was extended to women—a first in Europe.

However, this did not prevent another wave of Russian oppression from taking place from 1908 to 1914, resulting in the "Russification" of the Senate. Finland's autonomy was restored during the Russian Revolution of 1917. Later in the same year, Finland managed to break completely free from Russian rule.

INDEPENDENT FINLAND

The chaos of the October 1917 revolution in Russia gave Finland a chance to break free from Russian rule. On December 6, 1917, the Senate, under P.E. Svinhufvud, declared Finland an independent republic. Despite independence, Soviet troops remained in Finland, which was divided into Red and White camps. The Socialists, or Reds, who were anxious to retain Russian ties, gained control of the Social Democratic Party (SDP) and introduced their own Russian-style revolution at the end of January 1918. Taking over Helsinki and south Finland, they forced the Senate to flee to Vaasa in Ostrobothnia, where a White government was subsequently set up, controlling northern and central Finland.

In the civil war that erupted, the Whites received assistance from imperial Germany, with which they had close ties. In May 1918 the Whites, under General Carl Gustaf Mannerheim, won a major battle in Tampere that ended the civil war. Russia pulled out its troops from Finland. Germany then tried to move in to establish its sphere of influence firmly.

However, Mannerheim did not favor strong German links and moved to forge ties with the Allied forces instead. Mannerheim, who became Finland's head of state in December 1918 and held the title of "Regent," ratified the constitution on July 17, 1919, and Great Britain and the United States finally recognized Finland's independence. K.J. Ståhlberg was elected the first president of the Finnish republic that same year. In 1920 Finland and Russia normalized relations by signing the Peace of Tartu.

The Finnish constitution was a compromise between the republican and the monarchist camps. It gave the president much of the power wielded by the head of state under the previous constitution. Responsible for foreign policy, he was also made commander-in-chief of the armed forces and had the power to dissolve parliament. The Finnish parliament

General Carl Gustaf Mannerheim led his White camp to victory in the civil war that broke out after the declaration of independence.

was kept busy passing legislation in the first years of the new republic. Laws were passed introducing compulsory education and military service, freedom of speech and worship, freedom to form societies, and land reform.

There was a period of healing when Ståhlberg passed an amnesty act that granted pardon to those convicted of leading the Reds. The civil war wounds were further eased when the SDP was allowed to take part in elections in 1919; it later became the largest party in parliament. From 1926 to 1927 the Social Democrats went on to form the government. In 1929 the anti-communist Lapua movement was born, patterned after the Italian Fascists, a group that encouraged militarism and nationalism. The Lapua movement—which had wide support among peasants, who had suffered greatly during the worldwide Great Depression—carried out an armed revolt in 1932, but it was squashed and later outlawed.

In the meantime the Soviet Union, anxious to bolster the defense of Leningrad, demanded that Finland give up some of its territory and allow a Soviet base to be built on the Hanko peninsula. Finland refused. In August 1939 the Soviet Union and Germany secretly signed a Non-Aggression Pact that ensured German neutrality when the Soviet Union attacked Finland later in November.

Although Finland was ill-equipped and fought alone in the Winter War (1939–40) that ensued, it managed to survive for three-and-a-half months. The war ended with the Peace of Moscow, signed in March 1940. Finland gave up the Karelian Isthmus and the outer islands of the Gulf of Finland to the Soviets, who acquired a base on Hanko.

Finnish fears of Soviet intervention grew worse when the Baltic states were forcibly made part of the Soviet Union in August 1940. Isolated from the West and with Sweden remaining neutral, Finland leaned toward Germany. So when Adolf Hitler invaded the Soviet Union in June 1941, the Finns followed suit in what became known as the Continuation War (1941–44). Finland occupied Eastern Karelia on the other side of the border, with plans to annex it. However, there was no alliance with Germany and the Finns did not take part in the siege of Leningrad. Still, Great Britain, an ally of the Soviet Union then, declared war on Finland.

The statue of K.J. Ståhlberg, the first president of Finland, stands outside Parliament House in Helsinki.

The Soviets launched a massive counterattack. Helsinki was bombed and heavy fighting broke out on the isthmus. Finland withdrew from the war a year before Germany fell in 1943. In September 1944 an armistice was declared in Moscow with terms dictated by the Soviets. Finland returned to its 1940 border in Eastern Karelia and, in place of Hanko, the Porkkala Peninsula was leased to the Soviets for 50 years. Finland also agreed to pay war reparations and reduce the size of its army. German troops in Lapland refused to leave and the Finns had to force them out in a bitter battle that ended in the spring of 1945.

Finland suffered greatly from the Continuation War, with 65,000 dead and 158,000 wounded. Homes had to be found for 423,000 Eastern Karelians who chose to cross over the border to Finland rather than stay under Soviet rule. Despite the outcome, Finland was the only country on the losing side not to be occupied by foreign troops. This was thanks to Mannerheim, the former head of state and Regent, who had been

Germany attacked the USSR in June 1941. Finland took the opportunity to launch the Continuation War on the Soviet Union in a bid to retake its territory. The Soviet Union counterattacked and bombed Helsinki. Great Britain, allied with Russia, declared war on Finland in December. Finland withdrew from the Continuation War in 1942. Finland and the Soviet Union agreed to an armistice in 1944. Finland gave up more land to the Soviet Union and agreed to pay 300 million gold dollars (equivalent to $570 million) in war reparations to the Soviet Union. A peace treaty was signed between Finland and the Soviet Union in 1947, affirming the conditions of the armistice.

appointed the commander-in-chief of the armed forces in November 1939, a position he held during the Winter War and the Continuation War. At the end of the Continuation War, Mannerheim was appointed President of the Finnish Republic. However, he resigned in 1946 because of poor health and was succeeded by Juho K. Paasikivi, who pursued a policy of reconciliation with the Soviet Union.

In 1948 Finland signed a Treaty of Friendship, Cooperation, and Mutual Assistance with Moscow in which it agreed to prevent any attack on the Soviet Union through Finnish territory. Finland's aim to remain outside great power conflicts became the cornerstone of the Paasikivi line in foreign policy.

Over the years, Finnish external relations began to stabilize. Finland paid off its war debt on time, the only country involved in World War II to do so. As payment was in the form of industrial goods, Finland had to reorganize its production structure. Machinery was rebuilt and the process of industrialization sped up. This paid off in the long run as it resulted in rapid economic development of the country. Finland completed its war payments in 1952.

In 1956 the Soviets ended their 50-year lease of Porkkala naval base early and returned it to Finland. The same year, Finland was accepted into the United Nations and the Nordic Council. In 1956 Urho Kekkonen became president and actively pursued Finland's policy of neutrality.

MODERN FINLAND

In 1975 Finland's neutral position was boosted when it hosted the first Conference on Security and Cooperation in Europe (CSCE) in Helsinki. Renamed the Organization of Security and Cooperation (OSCE) in 1995, it is the world's biggest security organization with 55 European and Central

URHO KEKKONEN: ARCHITECT OF FINLAND'S MODERN DESTINY

In the 1950s, as Finland emerged from the shadows of the Soviet Union and took charge of its own destiny, there was one man who helped chart its future—Urho Kekkonen. He was a key figure in rebuilding the economy and maintaining the course of neutrality advocated by Paasikivi, a stand that became known as the Paasikivi-Kekkonen Line. It was a policy that the country followed for the next two decades, allowing it to be friendly with nations in both the North Atlantic Treaty Organization and the Warsaw Pact. He was one of the architects of the modern Finnish state and a very shrewd politician. Kekkonen was Finland's longest-serving president, from 1956 to 1981, and was previously prime minister for two terms from 1950 to 1956. He was succeeded by Mauno Koivisto, who also adopted the "active neutrality" stance.

Asian states as members, as well as the United States and Canada. In 1992 Helsinki again hosted the summit. Fourteen years later, in September 2006, the summit returned to Finland, this time to Tampere.

In 1995, together with Austria and Sweden, Finland became a member of the European Union (EU). It was another historic moment for Finland when it, together with 11 other EU member states, said goodbye to its own currency, the markka (MARK-kah), in favor of the euro on January 1, 2002.

In February 2000 Finland elected its first female president, Tarja Halonen. In March of the same year, it adopted a new constitution. In May 2002 a bill to construct a fifth nuclear power plant, the first in the country in 30 years and the first in Western Europe since 1991, was narrowly passed by the Finnish parliament. The move caused the Green League to opt out of the ruling government coalition in protest.

Finland elected its first female prime minister, Anneli Jäätteenmäki, in 2003 but after only two months in office, she resigned over a scandal involving political leaks. In January 2006 Tarja Halonen was reelected as president for a second term.

The Soviet Union recognized Finnish neutrality in 1989. After the Soviet Union broke up in 1990, the 1948 Friendship Treaty with the USSR was declared null. In 1992 a new treaty was concluded with Russia and involved no military agreements.

GOVERNMENT

FINLAND IS RELATIVELY YOUNG as an independent nation compared to other European countries. For 700 years, from the Middle Ages until 1809, it was part of the Swedish kingdom. It was considered the eastern part of the Swedish realm and its social, economic, legal, and administrative institutions were patterned after those in Sweden. After the 1808–09 war with Russia, Finland became a part of the Russian empire. It was run as an autonomous Grand Duchy under the Russian czar, who functioned as the Grand Duke. It was only on December 6, 1917 that Finland severed its ties with Russia and became a sovereign republican state.

THE CONSTITUTION

When Finland was an autonomous Grand Duchy, it had its own constitution and form of government, separate from the rest of Russia. This constitution, ratified on July 17, 1919, was replaced on March 1, 2000. The new constitution replaced all the previous constitutional acts. The most significant change with the adoption of the new constitution was the curbing of the powers of the president and the elevation of the role of the prime minister.

Finland is a parliamentary democracy; the constitution guarantees the rights of Finnish citizens, who are considered equal before the law, with individual rights and political freedoms enshrined. Ultimate power is in the hands of the people, who are represented by the *Eduskuntar*, which is the parliament.

The constitution spells out the separation of powers among the parliament, the government, and the judiciary. Legislative power is essentially the domain of the parliament, which also approves state finances. Governmental power is in the hands of the Council of State, comprising the prime minister and ministers for various government

In 1907 Finland became the first country in the world to elect women to parliament; that year, 19 out of the 200 seats in parliament were won by women, one of whom was feminist and former servant Miina Sillanpåå, who would remain in office for 40 years.

Opposite: **Senate Square at Helsinki.**

WHY DID FINLAND ADOPT A NEW CONSTITUTION?

Finland took 81 years to overhaul its 1919 constitution. Why did it take so long? The answer was simply because there was no pressure or need to do so, especially when the Finnish system allowed the use of excective laws to make amendments to the constitution to suit the times. In 1995 some changes were made to the constitution pertaining to basic rights. It was around this time, especially with Finland's integration into the European Union (EU), that the process of significant constitutional reform began. After all, most of the EU member states' constitutions were contained in one single constitutional act, whereas Finland's constitution had several acts. Also, there was a need to streamline procedures in keeping with those of other EU member states.

Finland became a member of the United Nations and the Nordic Council in 1955.

departments, as well as the Chancellor of Justice, who is an ex-officio member. The prime minister, who is elected by parliament, chooses his own cabinet ministers, but all ministers have to be formally appointed by the president. Judicial power is vested in the independent courts of law, the Supreme Court, and the Supreme Administrative Court.

There are 200 members of parliament and they are elected by direct vote for a period for four years. However, the constitution gives the president the right to dissolve parliament before the end of four years and to declare fresh elections. The new constitution allows for 12 to 18 electoral districts or constituencies from which members are elected to parliament. The autonomous Åland Islands has its own constituency represented by one member.

ROLE OF THE PRESIDENT

Until its revision in 2000, the constitution vested very comprehensive powers in the president. His role has since been reduced; although the president is still responsible for foreign policy and national security and is the commander-in-chief of the nation's armed forces, all other areas come under the purview of the prime minister, who is also responsible for EU relations.

Presidential authority in domestic politics is also much more limited than it used to be, with the prime minister now taking charge.

Still, the post of the president is regarded as prestigious. The president wields considerable power on official appointments and is the ultimate

RESULTS OF MARCH 2003 GENERAL ELECTIONS

Name of party	Percentage of votes	Parliamentary seats won
Finnish Center	24.7	55
Social Democratic Party	22.9	53
National Coalition Party	18.5	40
Left Alliance	9.9	19
Green League	8.0	14
Christian Democrats	5.3	7
Swedish People's Party	4.6	8
True Finns	1.6	3
For Åland in Parliament	0.2	1
Total (turnout 66.6 percent)	95.7	200

Source: Finnish Ministry of Justice

decision-maker on pardons. He also retains the right to declare elections; to call for emergency sessions of parliament and preside over its opening and closing (but he can no longer dissolve parliament if the prime minister has not made such a proposal); and to block legislation by applying his temporary right of veto.

The president presides over the Council of State, attending the ordinary sessions, when government decisions are made on legislative matters. During these sessions, the president makes a formal decision on the legislative bills to be put before parliament or whether to sign acts that have been passed by parliament. The president is not obligated to take into consideration the views of the prime minister or the majority of the Council of State, but in practice he usually does. All other meetings of the Council are conducted by the prime minister.

Martti Ahtisaari, a former UN diplomat, was elected the 10th president of Finland in 1994. He was a Social Democrat and was the country's first president elected by direct vote.

PRESIDENTIAL ELECTIONS

On January 29, 2006, Tarja Halonen (*right*) was reelected president of Finland for a second six-year term. This was the country's third presidential election by direct vote. Halonen is a member of the Social Democratic Party (SDP). She is the country's first female president and its 11th president, replacing Martti Ahtisaari, who had been president from 1994 to 2000. Halonen was the Minister for Foreign Affairs prior to her election (1995–2000) and had earlier served as Minister of Justice and Minister for Social Affairs and Health.

Political parties that had at least one member of parliament elected in the most recent parliamentary election can submit nominations for the presidential election. Also, anyone with proof of more than 20,000 supporters may run for election. In 2006, eight presidential candidates ran for president.

Under Finland's electoral laws, if one candidate were to receive more than half the vote during the election, which is traditionally held on the third Sunday in January, he or she would become the president. However, if no candidate received more than half the vote, a subsequent round of voting, called a run-off, would be held to choose between the two candidates with the most votes.

Since the first round of voting on January 15, 2006 produced no clear winner, a run-off was held on January 29. Halonen, the incumbent president, won by 3.6 percentage points; her opponent was Sauli Niinistö from the National Coalition Party (NCP).

All Finnish citizens aged 18 years and older have the right to vote. The elected president, who must be a native-born Finn, takes office on March 1 for a six-year term. The country's president can only serve for two consecutive terms, so Halonen will not be able to stand for reelection in 2012. The president lives in Mantyniemi. Located in Helsinki, it was the first official residence to be built specifically for the president and was completed in November 1993.

In 1992 Finland applied for membership to the European Economic Community.

THE COUNCIL OF STATE

Currently, there are 12 government ministries under the Council of State, which is headed by the prime minister. The prime minister and his ministers are appointed by the president and have to be native-born Finns. The prime minister's increased responsibilities under the new constitution include setting the agenda for meetings, settling tie votes, acting as president when the latter is out of the country or is incapacitated, and most importantly, dissolving the Council of State if he deems it unfit to govern.

THE ÅLAND ISLANDS

The Åland archipelago, comprising over 6,500 islands and skerries, lies sandwiched between Sweden and Finland. Only 65 islands are inhabited and they support a total population of some 26,800. Its capital and only large town is Mariehamn.

The demilitarized Åland Islands enjoy a special position for historical reasons. Since 1856, at the time of the Crimean War, the islands were recognized under international law as an unfortified area. Most of its people are traditionally Swedish-speaking.

The islands have been largely autonomous since 1920, a status that was reaffirmed in 1951 and again in 1993, when an Act on the Autonomy of Åland was passed by the parliament of Finland on January 1. The governor is the highest official and he represents the government of Finland in Åland. The islands also have their own provincial parliament with 30 members who are chosen in a general election every four years. The parliament has to approve any change in, or repeal of, laws of a constitutional nature and legislates on all matters that pertain to Åland.

A government body with up to eight members, headed by a chairman who is elected by parliament, carries out the administration of the Åland Islands. It is assisted by a regional civil service and six departments.

Each ministry has its own area of responsibility and is usually headed by a minister, though some ministries are headed by two. There are currently 17 ministers in the Council of State, excluding the prime minister. The Council decides on important state affairs. Many of the ministries have internal boards where senior civil servants meet regularly to take care of key operational issues concerning the ministry. Issues concerning more than one ministry would be discussed by the ministers, and strategic issues concerning the entire country would be addressed by the Council.

The town hall in Turku, the old capital.

LOCAL GOVERNMENT

Finland is divided into six administrative provinces: Åland, Eastern Finland, Lapland, Oulu, Southern Finland, and Western Finland. Each province has a governor who is appointed by the president and runs the State Provincial Office.

The State Provincial Office is the joint regional authority for the central government in the following areas: traffic administration, social and health care, police administration, education and culture, competition and consumer affairs, and judicial administration. The country is further divided into municipalities representing the local level of administration, which oversees community services such as schools and water supplies. Finland has 432 municipalities, of which 114 are cities.

Provincial governments have extensive powers as they are self-governing entities. They are responsible for the administration of their localities, with some funds being provided by the central government, although the provinces can levy taxes to raise money.

The highest office in local government is the municipal council, which is a decision-making body. The members, numbering 13 to 85 depending on the size of the population of the municipality, are elected directly by residents every four years. The councils vote for their own chairmen. Members of the executive committee—the municipal board—are also elected by the councils every two years. Administrative functions are carried out by statutory and voluntary committees appointed by the councils.

The municipal or town manager holds the highest office in local government. He is appointed by the municipal council and is answerable to the municipal board.

POLITICAL PARTIES

Finland's political parties campaign actively in elections at all levels—local, general (parliamentary), presidential, and even European parliamentary. Nine parties had members elected to parliament during the last general election, held on March 16, 2003.

Given Finland's proportional representation system—a system that deems that all voters merit representation and that all political groups ought to be represented in the legislature according to their strength in the electorate—multiple parties are the norm on the country's political scene and this has resulted in many coalition governments. For example, in 1995 the SDP won the greatest number of parliamentary seats, but with only 28 percent of the votes garnered, the SDP had to join with the NCP, the Left Wing Alliance, the Green League, and the Swedish People's Party (SPP) to form what has been dubbed the "Rainbow Coalition." In 1999 the SDP received 22.9 percent of votes, the CP 22.4 percent, the NCP 21 percent, the Left Wing Alliance 10.9 percent, and the Green League 7.5 percent, and so a similar coalition continued. However, in 2002 the Green League withdrew from government in protest over the building of a fifth nuclear power plant in the country.

On March 16, 2003, 18 political parties contested the general election. The CP won 55 seats in parliament, with slightly more votes (24.7 percent) than the SDP's 53 seats and 22.9 percent share of the vote. The CP formed a three-party governing coalition with the SDP and the SPP.

A Finnish policeman at a roadblock in Helsinki's main harbor.

Leading the opposition in parliament is the NCP, followed by the Green League and the Left Wing Alliance.

The prime minister is traditionally the chairman of the party with the biggest number of votes won in the general elections. Hence, Anneli Jäätteenmäki, the leader of the CP, became Finland's first female prime minister in April 2003. For the first time ever, Finland had women holding the two most powerful political positions in the land, as president and prime minister. However, Jäätteenmäki resigned two months later, over a political scandal about the leak of classified materials. She was replaced as prime minister by the Center Party's new chairman, Matti Vanhanen.

THE JUDICIARY

There are three levels of courts in civil and criminal cases. The first is the circuit court, or city court. The Court of Appeal is next in hierarchy. Last comes the Supreme Court, which is the highest judicial authority in the country. In the provinces, administrative cases are dealt with by

EVOLUTION OF FINNISH POLITICS

Finnish politics has continued to evolve in the 21st century; more political parties have emerged on the scene—some of them splinter groups from the traditional established parties, while others are single-issue parties. Dynamics have also changed. The Finnish electorate has become more prone to changing their allegiances to political parties while the traditional political parties are showing greater flexibility in forming governing coalitions.

Three of the largest political parties, the SDP, the CP, and the NCP, have dominated the political scene over the last 50 years, though no party has enjoyed a majority position. The SDP has the support of the urban working class, white-collar workers, some professionals, and small farmers; the CP represents rural interests; and the conservative NCP reaches out to urban professionals and the business community.

When political activity by Communists was legalized in 1944, the Communist Party of Finland was formed and it commanded significant support during the cold war. However, the collapse of the Soviet Union left the party in shambles and in April 1990 some of the former Communists formed the Left Wing Alliance, which also absorbed the Finnish People's Democratic League and the Finnish Women's Democratic League. The Left Wing Alliance has been involved in a number of coalition governments and lately it has been trying to move away from its association with Socialism and Communism, but Finnish voters still equate it with the former Communists.

One of the significant changes on the political party scene was the emergence of the environmentalist Green League, formed in 1989. The Green League opposed the market economy system, which it considered to be ecologically unsound. The viability of the party—it was part of the governing coalition from 1995 to 2002—represents a shift in the thinking of Finnish voters.

the county administrative courts; appeal cases are heard in the Supreme Administrative Court. There are special courts to handle issues such as housing, land rights, and insurance.

Presidents and members of the Supreme Court and the Supreme Administrative Court are appointed by the Finnish president on the recommendation of the courts. Judges of the circuit courts are appointed by the Supreme Court; the other members are nominated by municipal councils. The highest legal office is that of the Chancellor of Justice appointed by the president. The chancellor is also the highest public prosecutor, overseeing the provincial police superintendents, sheriffs, and municipal public prosecutors. He sees to it that government authorities comply with the law and perform their duties. The chancellor attends the meetings of the Council of State and determines the legality of any decisions made.

ECONOMY

FINLAND IS A HIGHLY-INDUSTRIALIZED NATION with a free-market economy. It enjoys a per capita output that is on par with that of the United Kingdom, Germany, France, and Sweden. Its main economic sector is manufacturing, with the main industries being wood, metals, telecommunications, electronics, and engineering. Trade plays a vital part in the Finnish economy, with total exports amounting to about 40 percent of its gross domestic product (GDP). Among its key exports are high-tech products, especially cell phones, and forest products.

Rapid industrialization began after the end of World War II, due to the need to pay heavy war debts to the Soviet Union. In just over 20 years, Finland became a highly-developed industrial country, with annual growth in its GDP averaging 5 percent between 1950 and 1974. Finland's GDP increased to nearly 6 percent in the boom years of the 1980s, but went into a tailspin when the country entered a recession at the start of the 1990s. The economic downturn resulted in a rise in unemployment. The value of the markka plunged by 25 percent when its ties with the European Economic Community (EEC), later renamed the European Union (EU), and the European Exchange Rate Mechanism (ERM) were cut and it was allowed to float in the market.

Nonetheless, Finns continue to enjoy a higher standard of living than many of their European neighbors today. Per capita GDP in 2004 was 28,643 euros, making it one of the world's highest and placing the Finns' purchasing power above average for Europe. In fact, the World Economic Forum named Finland as the world's most competitive country for three consecutive years, from 2003 to 2005. Its growth rate is also the highest among the Organization for Economic Cooperation and Development (OECD) countries.

Above: **Three Finnish women in their traditional costumes smile for the camera with an umbrella showing the European Union flag. Finland joined the EU at the beginning of 1995, and it became part of the European Monetary Union (EMU) zone in 1999. Finland's markka was replaced by the euro as the country's official cash currency in 2002, affirming Finland's commitment to the European economic integration process.**

Opposite: **The exterior of Finland's Stockmann Department Store in busy Helsinki. Stockmann has a total of seven stores in the country to date.**

AGRICULTURE AND FORESTRY

Farmers in Finland have always combined agriculture with forestry; in summer, they work in the fields, and in winter, they turn their attention to the forests, which are an integral part of their farms. With mechanization in the 1950s, these two branches of the economy lost workers to other developing sectors. Only 8.5 percent of the Finnish workforce work in agriculture and forestry, down from 46 percent in 1950, and only 7 percent of land in Finland is under cultivation.

Most of the arable land is concentrated in southern Finland and consists mainly of vegetable gardens and fur farms. The most important crops are wheat, barley, oats, potatoes, rye, sugar beets, and oleiferous plants. From the fur farms come mainly fox pelts, of which Finland is the world's second largest producer, and mink pelts.

Dairy farming is the most important type of farming in Finland, making up two-thirds of the income from farming. At least 33 percent of all farms are dairy farms, while 9 percent are devoted to beef production. Poultry farming is also significant; of the 6 million poultry in Finland, 74 percent are reared specially for egg production. Finnish exports include eggs, meat, and dairy produce, of which the most famous is Finnish Emmental cheese.

Since the entry of Finland into the EU in 1995, more farms have been converting to organic production, encouraged by subsidies given for such a conversion and compelled by the declining revenue from conventional farming. In 1989 there were only 373 certified organic farms in Finland; the number rose to more than 5,000 in 2002, representing 7.2 percent of all arable land under cultivation in Finland. Farmers are paid a conversion subsidy of 147 euros per hectare for five years, while those already engaged in organic farming receive a grant of 103 euros per hectare, also for five years.

The increase in organic farming is in line with the Ministry of Agriculture and Forestry's strategy launched in October 2001, targeting 15 percent of the arable land under cultivation in Finland to be used for organic farming by 2010. Emphasis is given to the development of organic animal production, organic cereals, horticulture, and food processing. Today, Finland is one of the leading countries in the EU to practice organic farming.

WHERE MONEY GROWS ON TREES

Finland's most important natural resources are its forests, which cover about 70 percent of the country. Of this, 61 percent is family-owned. Pine is the main species, accounting for about 40 percent of the annual growth rate, followed by spruce (37 percent), birch, aspen, and alder. Timber from the forests is used as roundwood in the sawmill, board, and plywood industries, or as fiber in the paper and pulp industries.

Due to improved forest management practices and forest improvement measures, the felling rate of trees is about 20 percent lower than the replacement rate of trees, thus ensuring the sustainability of the forests. In addition, forest protection programs have been put in place by the government. Today, 10 percent of Finnish forests are protected, higher than in any other European country.

Finland's forests produce high-grade wood. Over 90 percent of all products in its wood industry are exported, accounting for 20 percent of Finland's exports and contributing 8 percent to the country's GDP. Paper and pulp industries top the list. Finland is the second-largest exporter of paper and cardboard after Canada.

Trees subjected to the ravages of acid rain.

41

PAPER PRODUCTION

Finland is the second-biggest supplier of paper after Canada, accounting for as much as a quarter of the world's needs for printing and writing paper. Apart from paper, the forest yields lumber, plywood, pulp, paperboard, panel board, and other paper-related products.

Finland's forest industry companies enjoyed a combined turnover of about 40 billion euros in 2005. That year, paper and paperboard production was 12.4 million tons, making up 4 percent of global production, while pulp amounted to 11.1 million tons. Lumber and plywood production totaled 12.2 million cubic meters and 1.3 million cubic meters respectively.

INDUSTRY

Apart from timber, paper, and pulp production, the other main industries in Finland are engineering (including electronics) and metals, which make up nearly one-third of Finland's total output and also its exports. One out of every three industrial workers is engaged in these industries. Initially, industrial output went toward fulfilling Finland's war reparations to the Soviet Union. When these were fully repaid in 1952, the Soviet Union continued to be a market for Finnish metal and engineering products. Over the years, both industries have kept abreast with market developments and are now highly sophisticated, employing advanced methods of technology.

High-technology sheet steel and copper production are the main sectors of the metal industry, while the mechanical engineering industry turns out automated machines and equipment for the agricultural, forestry, and wood industries; forklifts and trucks; electrical and electronic goods; as well as other consumer products. Other products include special seagoing vessels such as icebreakers, luxury ocean liners, and oil rigs that are adapted for extreme climatic conditions.

Finland is also well-known for its high-tech and innovative industries, such as the production of telephone exchanges, mobile telephones, cars, and electronic consumer goods. The chemical industry has a 10 percent share of total industrial output. Apart from oil refining and fertilizers, the more important branches of the industry include techno-chemical and pharmaceutical production. There is also good demand for products such as textiles, clothing, leather, jewelry, decorative glass, ceramics, furniture, and cutlery. The textile industry, however, has undergone change due to the emergence of cheaper manufacturing bases, like China. Gone are the companies making cotton, wool, and other fabrics. The textile houses that remain, such as Marimekko, concentrate on the design and production of high-end fashion wear.

A cheese-filling press at an agricultural research center.

The energy industry in Finland is small. Only 30 percent of total consumption is produced domestically, and the country relies heavily on energy imports from abroad. Traditional sources of domestic energy such as hydroelectric power, wood industry waste, and peat are now supplemented by nuclear power from four stations. A fifth nuclear power plant is being built and is expected to be completed around 2008.

CONSTRUCTION

There was a construction boom in the 1960s and 1970s brought about by migration and urbanization as people moved from the countryside to towns. A huge housing program was drawn up and transportation networks such as roads, railways, canals, and harbors burgeoned. Nuclear power

Local public transportation in Helsinki relies mainly on buses, streetcars, and the subway.

stations were built to provide more electricity. Industrial development also resulted in the mushrooming of new factories and offices.

In the 1970s the construction industry accounted for 9 percent of the GDP, fueled by the building of 70,000 housing units a year. The 1980s saw a slowdown in housing construction to about half the annual rate and companies were forced to look abroad for contracts.

Since the 1990s there has been a further shakeup in the construction industry, with several building companies coming under Swedish ownership and others seeking global business opportunities.

TRANSPORTATION AND COMMUNICATIONS

Finland's northerly geographical location, its small but widespread population, and its extremely varied climate have all been a mixed blessing; these have placed a burden on the transportation and communications networks, but have also helped to boost their development.

The country has a network of 48,584 miles (78,189 km) of roads used by 2.8 million vehicles, 90 percent of which are privately-owned cars. Road transportation is supplemented by railways. There are 3,642 miles (5,865 km) of tracks; a quarter of these are electrified while the rest use diesel engines. Each major town has its own transportation network. In Helsinki, this includes suburban trains, buses, and the subway.

The Saimaa Canal, which was built in the 19th century, gives boats access to the lakes of eastern Finland. Other canals allow people, goods, and timber to be transported along lakes and rivers. Inland waterways, however, have been largely replaced by roads, although shipping is still important between the Baltic and Finnish lake districts.

Finland has a well-developed domestic air network, recognized as one of the best in Europe. There are 148 airports in the entire country, the most important being Helsinki-Vantaa Airport, which handles 90 percent of all scheduled international flights and over 10 million passengers a year. More than 100 scheduled and charter airlines serving 60 destinations operate via Helsinki. The national carrier, state-owned Finnair, has international links to major cities, including the United States, Japan, and China.

The railway station in Helsinki, a city landmark, was designed by Eliel Saarinen and built between 1906 and 1914.

Finland is a communications powerhouse because of Nokia, the world's largest producer of cell phones. The Finns enjoy a superior, fully-digitized telephone network and communications system. Automated telecommunications—instant communications without the need for human intervention—cover the entire country and landlines are available everywhere, except in the most remote locations. However, the most phenomenal growth has been in the cell phone sector, with nine out of 10 Finns owning a cellular unit at the end of 2002, as compared to only 7 percent 10 years ago. This percentage of cell phone ownership is one of the highest in the world. Finland's Internet usage is also one of the highest in the world, with 1.1 million Finns, or 230 out of 1,000 people, owning Internet accounts.

FOREIGN TRADE

Due to the relatively small size of the domestic market, foreign trade is essential to Finland. The main exports in the first half of the 20th century were wood and paper products. In the 1950s, metal and engineering

A bustling flea market at Helsinki.

The shopper will find a wide variety of beautifully designed crafts such as ceramics, glassware, and jewelry. The country is also noted for its leather wear, handwoven rugs, and carved wooden objects such as toys.

products took over as the chief exports because of huge orders from the Soviet Union. Today, Finland's main trading partners are the European Free Trade Association (EFTA), which it joined in 1961, and the EU, which it joined in 1995. With its growing integration with Europe, Finland has diversified its major exports to include products from the metal, engineering, clothing, electronic, and chemical industries. The export share of traditional forest-related products has declined to 40 percent, down from 69 percent in 1960.

Nearly half of Finnish exports go to EU countries such as Sweden, its largest trading partner, Germany, Britain, France, and Italy. Outside the EU, Finland's biggest trading partner is Russia, followed by the United States and Japan. Trade with Russia and other countries from the former Soviet Union declined after the latter's collapse, amounting to only 5 percent of total exports in 1995. This has since risen to nearly 9 percent.

TOURISM

Finland received 4.5 million foreign visitors in 2005. More than half of them come from Europe, with Sweden, Germany, and Russia leading the pack. The United States ranks sixth in terms of tourist arrivals, chalking up 208,563 overnight stays in 2005, a third of Sweden's 600,000. The tourist industry employs over 57,000 people and generates an annual revenue that makes up 2.7 percent of Finland's GDP, making it the country's fifth most important source of foreign income.

Although most visitors travel by air to Helsinki, many come by ship or car ferry from Sweden, as Helsinki is an overnight journey from Stockholm, the Swedish capital. Summer is the favorite season for travel

A TOWN NAMED NOKIA

One of Finland's biggest success stories is Nokia, the world's largest producer of cell phones. Indeed, the name Nokia is synonymous with Finland. This telecommunications giant has a state-of-the-art headquarters in Espoo, from which it conducts its global business. The company employs 60,000 people in 120 countries. One in three cell phone users in the world owns a Nokia cell phone.

Nokia was established as a wood-pulp mill in 1865 in a town called Nokia, named after a small black marten inhabiting the region. In the early 1900s, Finnish Rubber Works started a factory in the area, making rubber boots. After World War I, it acquired a majority share in the wood-pulp mill then known as the Nokia Company. It also acquired Finnish Cable Works, a maker of telephone and telegraph cables. In 1967 all three merged to become Nokia Corporation.

Nokia made its name in 1981 when it produced the first car phones for the international cellular mobile telephone network (NMT) in Scandinavia. In 1987 it made the world's first portable telephone, known as the NMT handportable.

That same year, Finland's economy was restructured due to a recession. Emphasis was placed on developing high-technology and research and development (R&D) was encouraged with state funding. Companies like Nokia benefited. In 1992 it sold off its non-core business to concentrate on telecommunications. Since then, the company has progressed to become the world's leading telecommunications equipment manufacturer. Apart from making cell phones, it also provides cell phone infrastructure and telecommunications equipment for various applications and markets worldwide. Today, Nokia is the biggest company in Finland, representing about 3.5 percent of its GDP and nearly 25 percent of all its exports.

in Finland, thanks to the warm weather and a full calendar of events, including several music and dance festivals. Lapland is a favorite tourist destination because it offers visitors a chance to experience the great outdoors, and visitors can also pan for gold in many areas. Lapland is also the official home of Santa Claus, and nearly half a million visitors descend on a small village just outside of Rovaniemi in Lapland, close to the Napapiiri, or Arctic Circle, to visit him and his elves at his workshop. Each year, since 1950, letters written by over 600,000 children from all over the world and addressed simply to "Santa Claus, Arctic Circle" have been delivered there.

Flights by Finnair, the national airline, connect Helsinki and the rest of the country to major European cities, the American continents, and Asia, making Finland very accessible. Traveling in Finland is easy, as English is widely spoken.

Finland has become highly visible in the international business and technological arena these days because of its leading position as a cell phone maker.

ENVIRONMENT

IN 2005 FINLAND WAS RANKED first in the world in environmental sustainability by a study jointly carried out by Yale and Columbia universities and presented at the World Economic Forum. The study measured 146 nations using the Environmental Sustainability Index, which ranks countries in areas such as urban air quality, past and present pollution levels, and the strength of environment regulation.

Yet Finland faced a different scenario just a generation ago. In the 1970s the country was facing the typical problems of an industrialized nation: declining biodiversity as a result of intensive forestry and agriculture; air and water pollution; and the pressing need to conserve energy, preserve nature, and control waste production.

The Ministry of the Environment was formed in 1983 to tackle environmental degradation in the country. In 1987 it published the National Report on Environmental Protection in Finland, outlining the state of the environment, identifying problem areas, and suggesting possible solutions.

Today, much has been done—national policy aims to improve the efficiency of energy resources by influencing the patterns of production and consumption, reducing the amount of waste, and cutting down on the use of energy and materials—but protecting the environment is still a major concern.

Above: **Fishing is one of the favorite pastimes of Finns. The country is committed to striking a balance between tackling the needs of a progressive and increasingly urban society and sustaining the lush expanse of forest and clear, tranquil lakes it has been endowed with.**

Opposite: **View of a lake on Åland Island.**

"We depend on
nature and the
environment for
everything. If we
allow our forests
and lakes to
become polluted,
our Finnishness
will disappear too.
The hearts of the
Finnish people lie
in the lakes and
forests. They
are our identity,
our capital,
and riches."

—Matti Arkko,
environmental activist

AIR POLLUTION

Air pollution was an inevitable problem the more Finland became industrialized. Not only were industrial pollutants posing a health threat, they were also causing acid rain, which can leach into water and soil and harm fish, plants, and wildlife. The worst pollutants during Finland's industrialization height were nitrogen and sulfuric acid.

In the past 20 years, through a number of measures to fight air pollution, Finland has significantly reduced harmful emissions from power stations, industrial plants, and motor vehicles. Sulfur emissions, for instance, went down drastically by 80 percent from 1980 to 1995. Nitrogen emission was reduced by 10 percent over the same period.

The measures adopted included cutting down on the use of industrial fuel, using more nuclear energy, and improving production methods in the pulp, paper, chemical, and metal industries.

Today, Finns enjoy better air quality than many other Europeans. However, two outstanding issues remain. One is the quality of urban air, which has not improved as rapidly as hoped. The concentration of fine particles from traffic emissions, industrial plants, and power stations still needs to be reduced. The second outstanding environmental issue is acid rain, which cannot be solved by Finland alone; the source of acid rain comes less from Finland than from its neighboring countries, and this cross-border pollution requires international cooperation to resolve.

In 2002 the Finnish government launched its Air Pollution Control Program, laying out a wide range of measures to cut down emissions from traffic, energy production, industry, agriculture, machinery, leisure boats, and the combustion of wood. The program also set maximum annual emission levels for sulfur dioxide, ammonia, nitrogen oxide, and other gases, to be met by 2010. The implementation of this program, which was designed to meet the EU National Emissions Ceilings Directive, involves international cooperation and, when implemented throughout Europe, will help to solve Finland's two outstanding issues.

FORESTS

From the air, much of Finland is a sea of green, covered by endless stretches of forest speckled by shimmering blue lakes. Forests cover almost three-quarters of Finland, the most densely-forested country in Europe. Finland's timber industry is one of the world's largest and forests are Finland's biggest resource. This has led to concerns about deforestation, the loss of biodiversity, the loss of recreational use of the forests, threats to natural habitats, and the problem of sustainability.

View of part of Finland's thick woods and quiet waters from Badhusberg hill.

To address this, Finland passed the Wilderness Act in 1991. Twelve wilderness areas in Lapland, totaling an area of 1.5 million acres (3.7 million ha), 5 percent of Finland's land area, were designated as protected areas. Since then, more protected areas, including old-growth forests, have been designated.

In 1997 a National Action Plan for Biodiversity was drawn up. Its key goal was to protect the country's biodiversity by preventing the depletion of habitats and natural organisms. The Action Plan was revised in 2005. In addition, the Forest Act and the Act on the Financing of Sustainable Forestry were both implemented in 1997 to prevent logging activities in a growing forest and to stipulate a timeframe for regeneration work.

A mobile saw mill is kept busy in a land where trees provide the raw material for many of the rural houses, as well as much of the furniture.

In 1999 the National Forest Program 2010 came into force, aimed at securing employment and income derived from forestry, ensuring the health of forests and biodiversity, and allowing people the right to enjoy recreational pursuits that only forests can offer.

The regulatory work of the Ministry of Agriculture and Forestry has enabled Finland to conserve its forests. The rate of deforestation in Finland today is low. It is estimated that Finnish forests have a total stock of 70.6 billion cubic feet (2 billion cubic m) of timber, enough to encircle the entire globe with a wall that is approximately 33 feet (10 m) wide and 16.4 feet (5 m) high. The rate at which the stock is regularly replenished—2.6 billion cubic feet per year (75 million cubic m a year) is higher than the annual rate of harvesting—2.1 billion cubic feet (60 million cubic m)—thus ensuring sustainability.

WATER PROTECTION

Finland has adopted an active water protection program targeted at improving and protecting the water quality of its lakes, rivers, groundwater, and the Baltic Sea. The underlying principle of the program is that none of these should suffer damage due to human activities.

According to a 2000–03 survey of Finland's waterways, the quality of Finland's inland waters was deemed generally good, with 80 percent of its lakes and 73 percent of its sea area graded either excellent or good. However, its rivers and coastal areas were not graded as well; only half of Finland's rivers were rated satisfactory, while 26 percent of its coastal areas were rated satisfactory or passable.

To improve the situation, a number of long-term strategies have been adopted; an act on river basin management was passed in 2004. The act calls for the creation of plans that would serve as guidelines on managing river basins to achieve a good state of surface waters and groundwater by 2015. The first of such plans will be ready by 2009.

In 2005 an action plan for the Program for the Protection of the Baltic Sea, also to be implemented by 2015, was approved. The program is aimed at reducing maritime traffic risks, decreasing risks from hazardous substances at sea, protecting biodiversity, and generally increasing awareness on environmental pollution.

An overall program to identify water protection targets and to spell out steps to be taken to protect them is also in the works, with national guidelines expected to be ready by the end of the year 2006.

About 10 percent of Finland's lakes are affected by acidification—a small figure considering the vast number of lakes in the country. However, many of the lakes are shallow, increasing their vulnerability to damage by acid rain.

NATURE AND WILDLIFE CONSERVATION

With more than 180,000 lakes, Finland has huge wetland areas that serve as habitats for birds and other wildlife. The main threats to nature and wildlife in Finland are habitat loss, pollution, and hunting. Placing curbs on these has been the key to saving some species from extinction. For example, there was a reduction in the number of wetlands in the 20th century due to peat mining and draining of the land for cultivation. In addition, 10 percent of wild plants in Finland are in peril and are highly endangered.

Since the 1960s, Finland has introduced a number of protection programs, including drawing up a network of protected areas with different biotopes for wildlife. These include national parks and nature reserves, waterfowl habitats, shorelines, and forest areas.

With an active conservation program, the white-backed woodpecker is off the endangered species list, although the Saimaa seal and the white-tailed eagle are still on the highly protected list.

Overall, however, Finland's nature is clean, according to a recent World Wildlife Fund report. Most of Finland's lakes are pristine and 50 percent of its peatlands are still in their original state. Many of its forests are untouched and there are areas in Lapland where few people have been.

WASTE MANAGEMENT

At one time, Finland had the dubious reputation of producing the largest amount of municipal waste per capita out of all the countries in Europe. An active waste management program has since improved the situation and Finland now produces 205 pounds (93 kg) of waste per capita each year, or 45 pounds (20.4 kg) less than the European average.

Between 2000 and 2003, an 11 percent decrease in waste generated was achieved, and Finland is working toward a progressive reduction.

Finland's waste management policy centers on preventing waste, reducing the amount of biodegradable waste and the emission of methane (a greenhouse gas), and increasing the rate of recycling as well as the safe treatment of wastes.

EVERYMAN'S RIGHT

The Finns have a much cherished tradition—the right of free access to land and waterways, regardless of ownership, and the right to pursue activities such as picking berries, fishing in lakes, or sailing, without the need to seek permission. They call this "everyman's right." It applies to Finns and foreigners alike.

A view of Helsinki's harbor.

Currently, 60 percent of Finland's waste is landfilled, while 27 percent is recovered for material and 9 percent is recycled into energy.

Each of Finland's 13 regional environment centers has its own regional waste plan.

ENVIRONMENTAL ADMINISTRATION

The role of preserving Finland's biodiversity and protecting its landscapes is undertaken by the Ministry of the Environment, which is also charged with promoting the recreational use of natural areas and ensuring the sustainable use of natural resources.

Under its umbrella of influence is the Finnish Environment Institute which focuses on environmental research and development. Thirteen regional environment centers look after the conservation of nature in their respective areas.

In addition, two other organizations are involved in conservation; Metsähallitus Natural Heritage Services is charged with monitoring and protecting threatened species in the wilderness and in the nature reserves, while the Finnish Forest Research Institute manages the forest research areas in some nature reserves.

FINNS

AS A NORDIC PEOPLE, Finns are generally expected to have blue or bluish-gray eyes, fair skin, and blond hair. While many Finns do fit this description, there are also many dark-haired and brown-eyed Finns, a result of the continuing influx of people throughout Finland's history.

Research has shown that three-quarters of the Finns' genetic stock is European in origin and the remaining quarter is Siberian. The European element is strongest in the western part of Finland and along the coast, the result of Scandinavian immigration. The Siberian element comes from peoples migrating to Finland from Russia.

ORIGINS

The first people in Finland are thought to have been the tribes that, after the Ice Age, moved westward into what is now Finland. At one time, most of Russia was inhabited by peoples speaking Finnish or languages related to it. These people were pushed west by invading Slavs. They were joined by immigrants from the Baltic regions, also speaking a Finno-Ugrian language, who started settling about 2,000 years ago, first in Hungary and Estonia, and later in Finland. These early Finnish speakers were followed by Germanic groups that crossed the Baltic from regions south and west of present-day Finland.

The wave of Swedish settlers began when Sweden embarked on its colonization of Finland around the first millennium A.D., starting with the Åland Islands and the island of Gotland and moving into the coastal regions of the Gulf of Finland and the Gulf of Bothnia. Today, Swedish Finns make up 6 percent of the population. They retain their own language and culture, but are Finnish citizens. Many others have blended into the ethnic mix that makes up Finnish people today. The Finns consider themselves to be European but are proud of their heritage, diverse ancestry, and language.

Opposite: **Young Finnish women in their traditional costumes at the Kuopio Dance Festival in Finland's Kuopio City. The Sami of Lapland and the Romany form the main minority groups in Finland, and foreigners, or immigrants, form barely 2 percent of the population.**

Finland is a fairly homogeneous nation. It has two official languages, Finnish and Swedish; 92 percent of the population is made up of Finnish speakers and 6 percent are Swedish speakers. In addition, 2.4 percent of the population are Sami- and Russian-speaking minorities.

Dogsleds are a time-honored method used by the Finnish people to move around in the wilds. The rides are popular with tourists as well.

FINNS MAKE STEADFAST FRIENDS

"The common characteristics are: resilience, inner strength, patience, determination... a liking for the old and well-known, and a dislike for the new... steadfastness in duty, respect for the law, desire for liberty, honesty... a Finn is known for his reserve, for his caution. He needs time to relax and get to know people, but when he does, he is a trustworthy friend," wrote Z. Topelius in *Finland in the 19th Century*.

"Finns are generally suspicious of outsiders because of centuries of isolation. They are also a shy people and until recently not many could speak English, so there was this language barrier with foreigners. But once you get to know a Finn, you will find he's trustworthy and will make a good friend," says Finnish banker Kai Heinonen.

Finns have changed—their reticence and self-deprecating nature have given way to a new self-confidence as Finland enjoys its standing as one of the most "wired" nations in the world, with one of the highest percentages of cell phone and Internet usage. Finland gave the world Linux, the first open source software operating system, which was pioneered by university student Linus Torsvald in 1991. Finland is also the home of Nokia, the world's biggest manufacturer of cell phones. Finnish youth are highly-educated and connected to the cyberworld. There are 42 personal computers for every 100 Finns while nine out of ten Finns own a cell phone. The Finns are also becoming more mobile as they increasingly venture out to the far-flung corners of the globe.

POPULATION GROWTH

The first records of the size of Finland's population appear in the 1750s and indicate that there were just under half a million people in Finland at that point in time. Finland's population rose to over 800,000 in 1800. The growth rate was rapid in pre-industrial times, as the numbers doubled to 1.77 million by 1870. It doubled again between 1870 and 1915 due to improved health conditions, medical care, and a drop in the death rate.

Children below the age of 14 made up slightly more than 17 percent of the population in Finland by the middle of 2006. In 1950 they made up a good 30 percent.

Since then, Finland's birth rate has declined; the size of the population was 4 million after World War II and 5.23 million in 2006. During the 1980s the government tried to increase the birth rate by offering incentives and benefits to encourage families to have more children. However, one-child families are still common. Out of the 600,000 families with children in 2004, 43 percent had only one child each, while 38 percent had two children; families with four or more children made up only 4.8 percent. In the year 2004 the percentage of live births (11 percent) to deaths (9.1 percent) resulted in a population growth rate of 1.9 percent. In 2006 the country's population growth rate was 0.14 percent.

The low birth rate has been offset by immigration, which helped to increase the population at a net rate of 1.3 percent in 2004, when 20,333 immigrants, mainly from Russia, Sweden, and Estonia, entered Finland, compared to 13,656 emigrants.

Apart from a low birth rate, the Finnish population is clearly aging. The proportion of the population under 15 years of age declined from

30 percent in 1950 to 17.5 percent in 2004, and later to 17.3 by the end of 2005. It was 17.1 percent by 2006. In contrast, the percentage of the elderly (age 65 and above) has doubled during the same period, from 7 percent in the 1950s to 16.2 percent in 2006. The average life expectancy for Finns is 79 years; the average gender-specific lifespan in the country is 82 years for women and 75 years for men.

POPULATION SPREAD

Finland is the third-least-populated country in Europe, after Iceland and Norway. Over half of Finns, or 53.5 percent, live in three southwest provinces that make up only 15 percent of Finland's land surface. The biggest town is Helsinki with 560,000 residents, followed by Espoo with 230,000 residents and Tampere, which is the largest inland town with 204,000 residents. About 82 percent of all Finns live in urban areas.

Finnish gypsies arrived in Finland during the 16th century when they were driven out of Sweden by the authorities.

The country's main towns lie in the south and southwest because of industrialization and the spread of commerce. After World War II, when Finland started to industrialize rapidly and people were freed from farming jobs because of mechanization, workers moved from the inland rural areas to the factories and offices in the southern region around Helsinki. In recent years, however, the migration of people from rural areas has stopped and urban growth has slowed down.

The number of Finns emigrating has also had an influence on population size. It is estimated that about 555,000 Finns have emigrated to Sweden since the end of World War II, though half of them returned to Finland later or moved to another country. Today, there are 200,000 first-generation Finns and 100,000 second-generation Finns living in Sweden. Other popular places for emigration include Norway, Germany, and the United States.

Finnish gypsies form the nation's largest minority ethnic group. Most of them live in the southern part of the country, where they continue to practice their age-old customs.

THE SAMI

The minority culture known as the Sami live primarily in the far north of Finland, as well as in neighboring portions of Sweden, Norway, and Russia. In Finland, there are estimated to be only 1,600 pure-blooded Sami today; intermarriage between Finns and Sami has been common for centuries, and increased dramatically in the 19th and 20th centuries. A great many people of mixed Sami-Finnish ancestry exist today, some of whom identify with the majority Finnish culture, while others view themselves as primarily Sami. As Sami in the south of Finland were eventually assimilated into the expanding agriculture-centered lifestyle of the Finns over the course of many centuries, the older livelihoods of hunting, gathering, and reindeer herding—the mainstays of Sami life for millennia—survived only in the remote areas of the north. The Sami of Finland speak several different but closely-related Sami languages, all of which belong to the Finno-Ugric language family.

A Sami man wears his people's distinctive native dress, rarely seen these days except on festive occasions.

Traditional Sami dwelling. Many Sami people now live in modern houses.

The Sami of Finland used to be known as Lapps. This term, however, is deemed somewhat derogatory and offensive. The word lapp *means a patch of cloth used for mending, suggesting poverty and tattered wear. So, Sami is the more acceptable term to use today.*

Some Sami people continue to live off the land, much as their ancestors did, and a small percentage are still nomadic reindeer herders. They are experts at hunting and fishing, and they raise large herds of reindeer, which they depend on for a living. Reindeer are used to pull their sledges and transport their goods; the reindeer also provide milk and meat, and their skins are used to make clothes and tents; the antlers of the reindeer are highly-prized and are carved into pieces of sculpture. The Sami sell souvenirs made from reindeer fur and bone carvings at roadside stalls along the northern highways. While valuing their traditional ways of life and arts, today's Sami are also open to modern technology and innovations: cars, mobile phones, the Internet, and other features of the modern world are as common among Sami as they are among Finns.

The traditional dwelling of the Sami is a tent that is shaped like a Native American tepee. Called a *goahti* (GO-ah-tee), it comprises a pole frame covered with reindeer skins. Inside, skins are also used to keep the ground warm, and in winter, woven wool rugs keep the tent insulated. Some Sami still use a *goahti* seasonally, particularly when following reindeer herds from their spring to summer grazing areas.

The Sami have a colorful traditional costume that is green, red, and blue. It is worn with an embroidered cap. The upturned moccasin-like shoes that they wear in the winter are made from reindeer fur; so are their gloves, leggings, and coats. Hay is placed inside the boots, and sometimes, the gloves, for warmth.

Rovaniemi is the gateway to Lapland. It has a Sami village where the Sami way of life and customs are demonstrated to visitors. One custom is the Sami welcome that involves drinking reindeer milk from a small ceramic cup and having the milk poured down one's back!

THE FINNISH NATIONAL DRESS

The colorful Finnish national dress is based on the regional folk dress worn by Finnish peasants in the 18th and 19th centuries. Today, it is worn mainly during family celebrations such as weddings, school and church events, and by those taking part in folk dances and choir performances.

The dress for men consists of a linen or cotton shirt, a vest, and a wool or cotton jacket teamed with a pair of trousers or knee breeches made from wool or chamois leather. Black leather shoes are worn with gray or black socks. A scarf is wrapped around the collar and tied with a single knot, and a belt with key hook and knives complete the look.

The dress for women consists of a skirt and apron with a bow tied at the back. The top is a laced bodice. A scarf, tied into a triangle, may be worn underneath the bodice or on top of it.

A headdress is usually worn. It can be a cap with a hard crown and lace, a white soft cap with lace, or an embroidered version of either one. A key hook hanging from the waistband and a pair of black shoes add the finishing touch.

There are craft schools that teach the making of the Finnish traditional dress to those who are interested.

A Finnish family in national dress, of which there are local and regional variations.

LIFESTYLE

FINNS ENJOY A HIGH STANDARD of living. As much as 68 percent of Finns live in homes they own and 16 percent live in housing provided by the government. The remaining live in rented homes. All this has been made possible by a housing policy adopted by the government in the 1950s to cope with the flow of people from rural to urban areas. All housing areas are required to have basic amenities and the less well-off are given low-interest, long-term loans of 15 to 20 years to buy homes of their own. In addition, students, the elderly, and families with children can apply for a housing allowance from the state to help them cope with the high cost of housing.

Since the deregulation of the financial sector in 1995, 90 percent of housing loans are principally administered by banks. However, interest rates are kept low at 3.5 to 3.8 percent. The Finns have the lowest rate out of all the countries that have adopted the euro as their national currency.

Left: **The Finns love nature and the chance to retreat to holiday homes in the peaceful green countryside. Nearly every lake, big or small, is dotted along the shores with tiny wooden cabins where Finnish families spend their vacations.**

Opposite: **Finns relaxing at an outdoor café.**

65

Families and friends sharing a meal at an outdoor bistro on a fine weekend afternoon in Helsinki.

FAMILY STRUCTURE

Older Finns lament that the influence of rapid modernization is leading to the demise of some customs and traditions. In the past, children would not leave home until they got married. Today, it is increasingly common for university students to live on their own and for couples to live together before marriage. But one family tradition is still strong—the Sunday lunch, when every family member gathers in the home of the parents to spend time together.

The typical Finnish family spends about 13 percent of its combined household income on food. Cars, leisure, travel, cultural activities, education, hobbies, and electronic products, especially high-tech gadgets, absorb another 40 percent of the family income. Virtually every household has a television set, a video cassette recorder (VCR), and one or more cell phones, while 47 percent of Finnish households own a personal computer.

As in many countries around the world, the traditional roles of men and women in the household have evolved into one of partnership, with family burdens being shared between husband and wife and critical decisions like the kind of schools their children attend or where the family should live being made jointly. Increasingly, men are getting more involved in bringing up their children and doing household work.

With the rise of Internet usage, the traditional family lifestyle has also undergone changes; the increasing use of technology has created social barriers, with some families interacting less often because children spend more time in their rooms using the computer to surf the Internet, play games, or watch videos.

A DAY IN THE LIFE OF A TYPICAL FINN FAMILY

As hired help is expensive, few families employ maids or domestic help. The wife does the household chores, with some help from the husband. She prepares breakfast and sees the children off to school before she and her husband leave for work. Lunch is eaten at school or at the workplace and the family gathers again for dinner at home. The day's evening meal is served at around 6:00 P.M. It is usually simple because no one has the time to prepare elaborate meals. The meal is kept light also because Finns tend to go to bed early. In the evenings, with a babysitter to look after young children, the parents can take time off to go to the movies, the theater, or a concert.

Families like to spend time together enjoying nature on the weekend.

The weekends are important for family time. Much time is spent enjoying the great outdoors—going for walks, jogging, or bird-watching. During the summer, many families spend weekends at their lakeside summer house fishing, sailing, having an outdoor barbecue, or enjoying their sauna, followed by a dip in the crystal-clear waters of the lake. In the fall, they go into the woods to pick berries and mushrooms or to admire the changing colors of the forest. During the winter, they go ice skating or skiing. There is more time over the weekends to cook elaborate family meals.

A young woman studies for her exams. Finnish women enjoy equal opportunities for education and employment, and many are highly educated. Women in Finland were the first in Europe to be entitled the right to vote and be active members of parliament.

Women make up almost 50 percent of the workforce. Many serve in public offices and head university departments and trade unions.

ROLE OF WOMEN

Finnish women are proud of their privileged status; in 1906 Finland was the second country in the world after New Zealand to give women the right to vote. Finnish women have the same opportunities as men to be educated at a university. They lead very independent lives, enjoy a status equal to men, and are allowed to keep their own family names, if they wish to, after marriage. Many women have double names, adding their husband's name to their own. Most continue working after they have families. It is estimated that women make up half of the student population in local universities, and about 70 percent of Finnish women work outside the home, of which 90 percent have full-time positions.

SAVVY YOUNG FINNS

In a survey carried out on the lifestyle habits of Finns aged between 15 and 24 years, 75 percent said they used the computer at least once a week while 60 percent surfed the Internet and sent e-mails frequently. Possessing the latest high-tech gadgets was considered "cool" and trendy, but when it came to purchasing such gadgets, Finnish youth displayed pragmatism when they said they would not blindly go for brand name products but would choose items for their price and quality. Increasingly, the young have been exerting influence over the purchasing habits of their families, especially when it comes to electronic consumer goods, because they are perceived to be more knowledgeable about such goods.

The current labor laws grant women 11 months of paid maternity leave, of which the first three months is termed maternity leave, and the remaining eight months is termed parental leave so that the parents can choose whether they want the mother or father to care for the child at home. A parental allowance is also given, although for the first 18 months this allowance only goes to the mother, after which it is applicable to either the father or mother, depending on who decides to apply for the parental leave. At the end of this period, there is a further entitlement of three years' unpaid leave from work, and the employer is obliged to keep the job open and available. In addition, a child home-care allowance is available until the youngest child turns 3 years of age.

Husbands are entitled to paid paternity leave of about three weeks. Every woman is given a "mother's box," which is a maternity gift from the government, upon the delivery of a child. The box includes a mattress that can act as a bed for the baby, a toy, and a gift pack of children's clothes, blanket, creams, hairbrush, and winter clothes. Cash is given if the mother prefers this, although the amount would be less than what is usually given in kind. All postnatal care is provided free.

In 2005 about 37.8 percent of the population was married.

The Equality Act of 1987 makes gender discrimination in the workplace a violation of Finnish law.

MARRIAGE

Most Finns prefer to get married in church, whether or not they are active churchgoers. Couples usually marry in spring or summer because of the favorable weather.

All children receive regular health check-ups under Finland's welfare system.

The man traditionally asks the father of his wife-to-be for her hand in marriage. There is no dowry. In the past, the dinner celebration, which was held after the church wedding, was hosted by the bride's parents at their home or in a restaurant. These days, the couple is likely to defray the costs or share them with their parents. The Finns believe that whoever has his or her hand uppermost on the knife when cutting the wedding cake will be the "boss" of the family. This also explains the custom of the bride and bridegroom rushing to be the first to step on each other's foot!

After the cutting of the cake, the dancing begins. The new couple has the first dance; the father of the bride then dances with her, while the bridegroom dances with his mother-in-law.

To mark the marriage, the parents of the bride also present gifts to the new couple. And on their first day as husband and wife, the bridegroom presents his wife with a gift of jewelry. In the past, the custom was for the bridegroom to give his bride a decorated wooden spindle so that his bride could weave clothes for the family. These days, if a spindle is given, it is used more as a decoration for the new home.

BIRTHS

The arrival of children is greeted with much fanfare in Finnish households. The father, who is often present during the delivery of the baby at a hospital, celebrates the occasion with his best friends the day after and gives out cigars to his colleagues at work.

When the mother and baby return home from the hospital, friends and relatives visit, bringing food, clothes, and other presents for the baby.

A kind of pastry known as *rinkelli* (RING-kel-li) is served with coffee and is also traditionally brought by visitors. One to three months later, a christening ceremony is held in the home. The baby usually wears a long dress made of lace, on which the names of those who have worn the same dress for christening are embroidered. This may include the baby's mother, father, or siblings.

The Finns traditionally leave their babies out on the open balconies of their homes to "get used to the fresh air," even during winter. They are warmly wrapped up, of course; it is believed that this makes them healthy.

Finland's infant mortality rate of 3.6 deaths in every 1,000 live births is one of the lowest in the world.

EDUCATION

Education is compulsory for children aged 7 to 16. They attend schools known as comprehensive schools until the ninth grade; they can choose to continue for another year into the 10th grade. After completing comprehensive school, students can attend upper secondary schools for three more years or enroll in a vocational school for two years. Further education is available at polytechnic schools for up to four and a half years to qualify for a higher education degree. These schools and polytechnics offer training in 25 trades and professions. Students can choose to qualify in the shortest period of time in the vocational schools as a car mechanic, for instance, or specialize in a longer course,

During the early years of schooling for young Finnish children, the country's comprehensive schools equip them with a general education. At the upper secondary level, academic subjects are studied unless the students are enrolled in a vocational school, where technical skills are taught instead.

Finland's first university was founded in Turku in 1640.

71

continuing at the polytechnic, that would train and qualify them as an engineer. Those studying in upper secondary schools can move on to universities to obtain a bachelor's degree and stay on, if they wish, to obtain a masters or a PhD. Finland has 20 universities, of which 10 are multidisciplinary, four are art academies, three offer economics and business administration courses, and three specialize in technology. There are 29 polytechnic institutions in the country.

Free schooling is provided up to the secondary level. For upper secondary education, students can apply for study grants or obtain low-interest loans. University students can turn to the state for grants or to the banks for state-guaranteed student loans. University students enjoy subsidies on health care, meals, and student housing.

A teacher minding her preschool charges at a day-care center.

PRESCHOOLS

Education for preschool children is voluntary. In practice, as more than three-quarters of mothers of preschool children are working, many toddlers end up in municipal day-care centers or in the private homes of approved babysitters, where some form of teaching is given. However, some children attend preschool classes that are part of comprehensive schools. The proportion of six-year-olds attending preschool is about 90 percent.

The Ministry of Social Affairs and Health and the local authorities work together to place young children of working parents into day-care centers and homes. Since 2001, it was decreed that all children had the right to preschool education and that this would be provided, free of charge, within the framework of day-care, wherever possible.

THE READING HABIT

Finland has one of the highest literacy rates in the world. The Finns are avid readers who purchase much of their reading material and also make good use of an extensive network of free libraries, borrowing, on the average, 20 books and audio book recordings per person per year. To support this habit, there are about 1,000 public libraries, 800 research libraries, which include 600 scientific libraries offering 15 million books, and a fleet of 200 mobile libraries. These libraries serve 18,000 neighborhoods throughout the country. The libraries have over 40 million books and 3.5 million non-book items such as DVDs, CD-ROMs, video cassettes, and audio book recordings.

Labor policy is regulated by law to protect both employers and employees. A standard employment contract covers working hours, annual vacation, and social benefits. Salaries and general wage increases are negotiated yearly.

SOCIAL SECURITY

Finland is a welfare state that provides for the basic needs of its citizens. It has a well-established form of social security, with working Finns paying high taxes to fund the various programs under the system, such as health-care benefits, protection for workers, and old-age pensions. There are special family benefits as well, including paid maternity leave, child allowances, and free schooling, plus special programs that cater to the needs of the elderly and handicapped. The country's social security system is one of the best in the world, protecting Finns against a gamut of possible social risks.

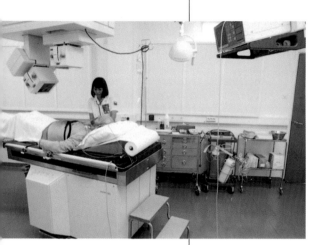

Most hospitals are government-run and the cost of treatment and medicine is heavily subsidized.

HEALTH CARE

All residents in Finland are covered by a generous health-care plan. A nominal fee is charged for medical care, X-rays, laboratory fees, physiotherapy, and hospital treatment. Expenses incurred from a hospital stay are reimbursed after a minimal deduction. Patients pay part of the cost of prescribed medicines.

Workers in Finland receive an allowance of up to 80 percent of their salary for each day that they are ill, and for those out of a job, a minimum daily allowance is also given. The cost of private medical care is also partially reimbursed. War veterans and those born in 1956 and after are entitled to free dental treatment.

A WELFARE STATE

Parents with children under the age of 17 are given child allowances. Those with children younger than 3 years of age receive an additional child home-care financial package. Families with handicapped or very ill children under 16 are given home-care assistance.

Trade unions operate voluntary unemployment benefit funds which members can draw from if they are laid off work. The funds are provided by the state, employers, and from contributions of the members themselves.

There is a maximum annual amount that can be paid as an unemployment allowance for a period of three years. Workers not covered by union funds are paid an unemployment allowance by the state to meet basic needs.

In Finland, even those who have never worked receive a national pension once they reach the retirement age of 65. This applies to both men and women. In some occupations, the retirement age may be lower.

The national pension is based on the wealth and income of each individual. For those who have worked before retiring, an employment pension linked to their previous earnings and number of years worked is also payable. The employment pension is paid only after 40 years of work. The earnings-related pension used to be capped at a maximum of 60 percent of the last-drawn salary but this limit was eliminated in 2005 as it discouraged people from working once they had reached this maximum. If a person receives a large employment pension, his national pension will be smaller.

An old man in a hospital that specializes in providing care for the elderly.

CARE OF THE AGED AND THE LAST DAYS

The elderly accounted for 13 percent of the total population of Finland in the early 1990s. Like other European countries, Finland's population is increasingly weighted toward the elderly.

The elderly in Finland prefer to be independent of their families, living in apartment blocks built specially for them so that they can get together with people of their own age. Municipalities also extend some help by arranging services such as cleaning, shopping, and cooking for a token fee. They also organize senior citizens' centers for the elderly to meet and obtain information. For those too old to look after themselves, there are senior citizens' homes.

The Finns prefer to have their elderly spend their last days in a hospital that can try to make their stay as comfortable and painfree as possible.

As with marriage, the majority of Finns prefer to have a Christian burial even if they had never been active church members.

RELIGION

FINLAND HAS TWO STATE RELIGIONS—the Evangelical Lutheran Church and the Orthodox Church. About 84.2 percent of all Finns belong to the Evangelical Lutheran Church, 2.2 percent to other Christian denominations, and the rest profess no particular faith or religion.

With strong influences from Russia and Sweden throughout its history, Finland has had to contend with the efforts of each side to establish not just their political spheres of influence, but also their religious cultures: the Roman Catholic Church from Sweden and the Byzantine Orthodox Church from Russia.

THE ROMAN CATHOLIC CHURCH

Christianity began to arrive in Finland around the end of A.D. 1000, but it was not until the middle of the 12th century that the Roman Catholic

Left: **Some religious paintings and iconography in Temppeliaukio rock church in Helsinki.**

Opposite: **The Lutheran Cathedral at twilight. The cathedral, with its distinctive dome and columns, stands in Helsinki's Senate Square. It was designed by C.L. Engel, who did not live to see it completed in 1852.**

A church on Turku Market Square shows the cruciform style.

Church managed to gain a foothold in southwest Finland. This was largely the result of the first crusade waged by King Eric of Sweden and Saint Henry, the bishop of Uppsala, to spread Swedish influence through missionary work.

The Roman Catholic Church used ritual, pomp, and pageantry in ceremonies to convert the nature-worshipping Finns. Masses were conducted mostly in Latin except for the Lord's Prayer, the Creed, and salutations to the Virgin Mary, which were said in Finnish. Incense, holy water, and other religious items were used for all ceremonies.

The first Finnish churches were built from logs. But when Catholicism took root, these churches were replaced by rough-hewn stone churches that were decorated with brick gables and shingle-covered, steeply-pitched roofs. These churches soon became an integral part of the landscape in southwest Finland and the Åland Islands. In the 13th century, Finland's only cathedral was built in Turku, which became the seat of the bishop.

In the 17th century the basilica type of architecture was replaced by a cruciform ground plan (shaped like a cross), with the altar and pulpit situated near the intersection to allow the congregation a better view of church proceedings.

THE REFORMATION

The Reformation, a Christian movement that challenged the authority of the Catholic Church, reached Finland in the 1520s. It spread in a gentle manner in Finland, unlike the way it was introduced to its Scandinavian neighbors, especially Norway, where reforms were pushed through regardless of opposition. The break with Rome took place in 1528 when Martinus Skytte was made the new bishop of Turku without seeking the approval of the pope, as was required by canonical law.

The use of Latin in church services was replaced by Swedish and first used in 1531 in Turku Cathedral. By the end of the 1530s bilingual services in Swedish and Finnish was the norm in churches. In general, there was no opposition to the changes brought about by the Reformation. Many did not understand the significance of the reforms, though some did initially miss the ceremonial aspects associated with the Catholic liturgy.

The educational ties with southern Europe's old universities and cultural centers ended with the Reformation. Finns were now sent to study in places such as Wittenberg and Rostock in Germany, and Prague in what is now the Czech Republic. In 1642 a Bible in Finnish was finally produced.

Frescoes with religious motifs in a medieval church in Espoo.

SPEARHEADING THE MOVEMENT

In the 1500s Finland lacked a university of its own, so its best students were sent to further their studies in other parts of Europe. The Finnish scholar Mikael Agricola, for example, studied at the University of Wittenberg in Germany under Protestant reformer Martin Luther. Agricola returned to Finland and introduced the revolutionary teachings of Luther and the Protestant Reformation to the Finns.

The towers of Johannes Church in Helsinki.

THE COUNTER REFORMATION

There was a brief resurgence of Catholicism coinciding with the reign of the Swedish King John III, in 1568. This Counter Reformation was the work of the Catholic Church in the newly-Protestant countries of Europe. It started when the Jesuits became dominant in Stockholm Theological University. At the same time, John III favored bringing back some features of Catholicism, especially the ceremonial aspects. He came up with a blend of the two religious doctrines to be used in the Swedish empire, submitting it to the pope for approval. The plan was rejected, as some of his suggestions, such as allowing priests to marry, were controversial.

There was also opposition to John III's religious policy in Sweden and Finland, especially when he came up with the *Red Book*, which outlined more Catholic forms of worship to be adopted in churches.

The Counter Reformation movement did not gain much headway and the Protestant Church became firmly established in the latter part of the 16th and early 17th centuries. Legislation was passed prohibiting citizens from holding onto variants of the Catholic and Protestant faiths, such as sacramentalist, Zwinglist, Calvinist, Anabaptist, or any other heretical doctrines. In 1617 the state went further by issuing a law that forbade conversion to Catholicism. Those who did so risked being banned from the country.

THE ORTHODOX CHURCH

The influence of the Orthodox Church was confined to the areas in Finland where Greek Orthodox culture had taken root since the Middle Ages. The appointment of Isak Rothovius as Bishop of Turku in 1626 gave the church a boost, as he was a supporter of Orthodox thinking.

The Orthodox Church was most dominant in the east, in Karelia, which looked toward Russia for spiritual guidance. For a time, during a movement to convert the Orthodox population to Lutheranism, many Orthodox followers crossed over the border to Russia to practice their faith. When Finland became an autonomous Grand Duchy of Russia from 1808 to 1917, the presence of the Orthodox Church became even more pronounced. There was an Orthodox church or chapel wherever a Russian garrison was stationed.

The Russian Orthodox Church flourished during the Russian occupation of Finland in the 18th century.

Today, the Orthodox Church continues to thrive. It is the second-largest church in Finland with a membership of about 60,000.

THE CHURCH'S ROLE

Present-day Finland is predominantly Lutheran with about 600 Lutheran parishes and more than 4.3 million Lutheran followers, making it the third largest Lutheran congregation in the world, after the Netherlands and Germany. The parishes are grouped under nine dioceses, each of which has its own bishop. Among the nine dioceses, one is Swedish-speaking. All bishops are appointed by the Finnish president from a shortlist

Women priests are a relatively new presence in Finland.

provided by each cathedral chapter, which is a local body of church members who advise the bishop and help him oversee cathedral issues. Turku continues to be the seat of the archbishop.

There is a strong individualistic element in Finland's largely Protestant society, but the church still plays an important role in Finnish lives. More than 90 percent of all children are baptized and confirmed, and all Finns make it a point to attend church at some time or other in their lives. Whether or not they are active church members, being married in church is considered obligatory, as is being buried according to religious rites.

THE SYNOD

The Church Assembly, or Synod, is the highest decision-making religious authority in Finland. One-third of its members are drawn from the clergy and the rest from the lay public. The Synod looks after the operations of the churches and their finances. It also proposes changes to the Ecclesiastical Act, which must be approved by parliament.

The ordination of women priests—after a controversial debate—was consented to by the Synod in 1986. Parliament approved the amendment to the Ecclesiastical Act in 1988, the year when the first graduating class of women theological students was ordained. The office of bishop is also open to women.

FREEDOM OF RELIGION

As in many European countries, the church in Finland is no longer associated with the state. Except for the right to levy taxes, the church is virtually independent. The church tax, paid by church members as well as companies, is collected on its behalf by the internal revenue department. The money pays for communal services provided by the church, such as the keeping of birth and death registers and the maintenance of cemeteries.

Finland granted its citizens complete freedom of religion in 1923. Depending on their beliefs, parents may have their children study religion at school or not.

The third most important church in Finland is the Pentecostal movement with a congregation of 50,000. The other churches are much smaller in membership and include Jehovah's Witnesses, Seventh-Day Adventists, the Finnish Free Church, and the Roman Catholic Church.

The Orthodox archbishop blesses the souls of the deceased in a ceremony held at a cemetery.

LANGUAGE

FINLAND IS BILINGUAL. Its two official languages are Finnish, spoken by 92 percent of the population as their mother tongue, and Swedish, spoken by 5.5 percent who live mainly along the coast in the archipelago and around the Gulf of Bothnia. In Lapland, about 1,600 people speak Sami, which comprises several languages, and in the south, about 5,500 gypsies have their own language. In 1991 Finland passed a language act that accorded the Sami languages official status, with the right to be used in government service.

With only 5.2 million people in the world speaking Finnish and with very few foreigners knowing the language, which is difficult to learn, many Finns have learned to speak other languages—usually English, German, or some other European language.

Before the 19th century, Finnish poetry and folk tales reflected a strong Swedish influence. The Finns' pride in their own language and culture began to take root only in the latter half of the 19th century, thanks to the efforts of scholars like Elias Lönnrot, creator of the Kalevala *and one of the first university professors of Finnish, and J.V. Snellman.*

Left: **A road sign for motorists. Finnish as a language has its origins in eastern and northern Europe.**

Opposite: **Friends chatting at midday on the steps of the Lutheran Cathedral built in 1852 on Helsinki's Senate Square.**

A boy reads at a day-care center. Finland has one of the highest literacy rates in the world, and Finns are fond of reading. This can be attributed to a tradition dating to the Church Law of 1686, which forbade marriage to anyone who could not read.

Although it is part of Europe, Finnish has nothing in common with other European languages as it is not Indo-European in origin. Yet, there are some words in Finnish—about 15 percent—that have been taken from the Baltic, Slavic, Swedish, Russian, and Germanic languages, and many Finnish words are derived from French and English. In recent years, especially in the areas of technology and science, English has become a very important source of new terms.

Finnish is closely-related to Estonian and, to some extent, Hungarian. Like these two, Finnish belongs to the Finno-Ugric group of languages, which is spoken by 23 million people worldwide. Sami is distantly related to Finnish and is not easily understood by Finns.

Unlike the English alphabet, the Finnish alphabet has three extra letters: Å, ä, and ö. Instead of five vowels, it has eight: *a*, *e*, *i*, *o*, *u*, *y*, *ä*, and *ö*. Finnish words tend to use many vowels and few consonants.

PRONUNCIATION

Finnish vowels are pronounced the same way as in English except for the following:

y is pronounced like the German *u* with the umlaut.

ä is like the *a* in *fact*.

ö is pronounced like the second *e* in *theater*.

If a vowel occurs twice, as in *aa* or *ii*, there is a slight drag in the pronunciation, such as in *aah* or *ee*.

Certain consonants are pronounced differently from those in English:

z is pronounced as *ts* and can be written as such.

v and *w* are considered the same letter.

b has a weak sound except at the end of a closed syllable, when it is pronounced with more force, as in the German *ch* in *ich*.

j is pronounced like *y* in *yellow*.

r is rolled.

Double consonants, such as *kk* in *Keskiviikko* (KES-kee-VEEK-oh), which means "Wednesday;" or *aa* in *saari* (SAAH-ri), meaning "island," are held longer. *Ng* and *nk* are two syllables and are pronounced as *ng-ng* and *ng-k*. For instance, *vangit*, which means "prisons," is pronounced "VAHNG-ngit." The syllable *np* is pronounced as *mp*; so *olenpa*, meaning "I am," becomes "OH-lem-pa."

Finns chatting and discussing the day's affairs at an outdoor café.

Finland's printed media has a history dating from 1771, when the first newspaper was published. The oldest newspaper in Finland is the Swedish-language Abo Underrattelser, *first published in 1824. Present-day Finland has as many as 50 different types of newspapers, national as well as regional, and six Swedish-language newspapers.*

The Finnish language does not use articles of speech such as *a* or *the*. Prepositions are rare and the language does not distinguish between male and female pronouns—both are referred to as *hän* (hahn), or "hand." As in French, Spanish, and other European languages, the Finns have two different ways of saying "you:" the informal *sinä* (see-NA) when addressing close friends and relatives and the formal *Te* (tay) when speaking to acquaintances or at a professional level.

FORMS OF ADDRESS

Often, the Finns do not use forms of address such as Mr., Mrs., or Ms. Instead, they tend to address people according to

Three Finnish children using multimedia resources at the Vapriikki Museum Center at Tampere. Language is an important part of the curriculum in Finnish schools.

their profession. For instance, a Mr. Rotko who is the managing director of a bank will be addressed as *Maisteri* (MAIS-ter-ri) Rotko, meaning "bank director Rotko."

AN UNUSUAL LANGUAGE

The Finnish language has been acknowledged as one of the most difficult to learn. Finnish is different from most of the other European languages, although its melodious intonations may remind the visitor of Italian. A lot of vowels are used in Finnish. Diphthongs (that is, *ai, ei, iu,* and *ou*) occur very often. Consonants are so uncommon that

Finnish words never begin with two consonants. For instance, the Germanic word *strand* (SCH-t-ra-nd), meaning "shore," becomes *ranta* (RAHN-ta) in Finnish, with two consonants dropped.

Words in Finnish can have many different forms—as many as 15 in some cases. In contrast, Latin words only have six different forms. The form of a Finnish word depends on the context. For example, *talo* (TAH-lo) means "house." To say "in the house," the word changes to *talossa* (TA-lo-sa), and to mean "of the house," it becomes *talon* (TA-lon).

For a time, Finnish as a language was threatened when, during periods of foreign occupation, languages such as Swedish and Russian were used instead. Despite much pressure, the patriotic Finns stuck to their own language. Like many other languages, however, new Finnish words have evolved over time to reflect outside influences, especially English. Thus, there is *rokkimusiikki* (ROK-kee-MOO-see-kee) for "rock music" and *bandi* (BAHN-dee) for "band." While some Finnish words are a bit of a tongue

A prohibition sign forbidding loitering, excessive drinking, pets, and smoking in an indoor market in Turku.

twister, there are others one would be able to pronounce easily and even recognize their meanings right away:

hotelli (HO-tel-li)	hotel
motelli (MO-tel-li)	motel
auto (AW-toh)	car
taksi (TAK-si)	taxi
dieseli (DEEY-sel-li)	diesel

To say "yes" in Finnish, one says "*kyllä*" (KOO-la). The word "no" is *ei* (ay), while "thank you" is *kiitos* (KEEH-tos). For "please," one says "*Olkaa hyvä*" (OHL-kaah HOO-vah) and "goodbye" is "*näkemiin*" (NA-kem-een).

AGRICOLA—FATHER OF WRITTEN FINNISH

The man acknowledged to be the father of Finnish literature is Mikael Agricola (1510–57), who created the Finnish written language. In the Middle Ages, the literary language was Latin. Later, Swedish prevailed because of Sweden's domination of Finland, especially with the founding of the Turku Academy in 1640, where professors initially wrote in Swedish. The Lutheran Reformation in the 16th century gave a boost to the Finnish language, for it propounded that all religious writings, especially the Bible, be written in the people's own language.

It was Agricola who translated the New Testament in 1548 and the Psalms of David in 1551. He was among the first batch of students at the new University of Wittenberg to study under German Protestant

A statue of Mikael Agricola sculpted by Emil Wikstrom in 1908.

reformers Martin Luther and Philipp Melanchthon after the Reformation found its way to Europe. After three years, he returned to Finland, where he was appointed a schoolmaster in Turku, then a member of the cathedral chapter, before becoming a bishop in 1554.

His first work in the Finnish language was the Finnish ABC book, *ABC-kiriai*, in 1543 followed by the Book of Prayer from the Bible that same year. The Finns are truly indebted to him, for it was Agricola who created the written Finnish language, coining many new words that are still in use today. Thanks to his pioneering efforts, the complete Bible was finally translated in 1642, an enormous task that took nearly a century.

The Finnish language has words borrowed from the Swedish, German, Baltic, and Slavic languages and, more recently, from English.

TOVE JANSSON—CREATOR OF THE MOOMINS

One of Finland's best-known writers is Tove Jansson (1914–2001). Her books about "little trolls" and their adventures in Moominland are favorites among children in Scandinavia and has even gained a following in Japan. Although Jansson's stories are for children, they often address grown-up themes, like the cold war or facing a mid-life crises. She was awarded the Hans Christian Andersen Award in 1966 for her contributions to children's literature. Jansson, whose father was a sculptor and mother an illustrator, was also an accomplished painter. A member of the Finnish-Swedish minority, her books were originally written in Swedish and have been translated into 33 languages. They are the most translated works of Finnish literature after the *Kalevala* and books by Mika Waltari. A theme park devoted to the Moomins exists outside Naantali, near Turku.

ARTS

THE OLDEST FINNISH LITERATURE consists of folk poetry, songs, proverbs, and legends that have been passed down from generation to generation by word of mouth. In other areas of artistic achievement, Fredrik Pacius composed the national anthem, *Our Land*, while Jean Sibelius wrote orchestral music, with *Finlandia* being his best-known work.

RUNE SINGERS

A 25-line commentary against the plague, written in 1564, is said to be the earliest folk poem written down in the Finnish language. Prior to that, stories were remembered through runes—folk poems that were sung. The skills of rune singing were often passed on in the family, and a singer usually learned the lines from his or her parents. Tunes played on the harp-like *kantele* (KAHN-tay-leh), an ancient Finnish instrument, accompanied the poems.

Rune singers were primarily women, although the men tended to sing epic poems and women, the lyrical ones. In the 19th century, many of the rune singers were old and some were blind, like the well-known Miihkali Perttunen, the son of Finland's greatest rune singer, Arhippa Perttunen, who contributed one-third of the material for *Old Kalevala*.

MODERN LITERATURE

A literary figure in the 19th century who was influential in shaping the Finnish national identity was Johan Ludvig Runeberg (1804–77). The Swedish-speaking Runeberg lived in the rural backwoods of central Finland, working as a tutor for a wealthy family on a country estate. He had opportunities to observe the life of rural peasants, romanticizing them in his first poems.

Above: **A monument to honor the great Finnish composer Jean Sibelius. Built by Finnish sculptor Eila Hiltunen between 1963 and 1967, it weighs 24 tons and is located in Helsinki. About 32.8 feet (10 m) from the Sibelius Monument is the face of the composer himself.**

Opposite: **The sculpted head of Jean Sibelius.**

THE KALEVALA AND ELIAS LÖNNROT

The *Kalevala* is recognized as Finland's national epic poem. It was compiled from Finnish folklore by Elias Lönnrot (1802–84), who recorded the folklore from rune singers. The work took several years to finish and represents the first written collection of Finnish folk poetry.

Lönnrot was born into a poor family in a small village west of Helsinki. He learned to read at home and only started school when he was 12. He went on to study medicine and became a doctor, but his passion was collecting Finnish folk songs. It was in the early 1830s that he had the idea of compiling a series of miniature epics based on the exploits of heroes, such as Väinämöinen, who were featured in folk poems. His compilation was published in 1833 as the *Proto-Kalevala*.

In 1834 Lönnrot was granted a scholarship by the Finnish Literature Society to travel and collect more folklore. The result was *Old Kalevala*, published in 1835. As time went on, Lönnrot gathered even more poetic material and all these were compiled into the second edition *Kalevala*, which appeared in 1849 and has since been considered the foundation of Finnish culture. The "new" *Kalevala* had 50 cantos, a canto being a main division of a long poem. It stimulated interest in Finnish history and later, at the end of the 19th century, became a symbol in the drive for national independence. The epic has been translated into 43 languages and is the best-known work of Finnish literature.

Lönnrot collected much of his material in Karelia, where rune singers can still be found today. His work was a boost to the local arts. It sparked interest in the systematic collection of folk poetry, a task that is now undertaken by the Folklore Archive of the Finnish Literature Society, the biggest of its kind in the world.

I have a good mind
take into my head
to start off singing
begin reciting
reeling off a tale of kin
and singing a tale of kind.
The words unfreeze
in my mouth
and the phrases are tumbling
upon my tongue they scramble
along my teeth they scatter.

— The opening lines from the *Kalevala*, translated into English by Keith Bosley, 1989

The Elk Hunters, written in 1832, rose to the status of a national epic. It was among the first works to be translated into Finnish by the newly-launched Finnish Literature Society. But it was Runeberg's *Vänrikki Stoolin Tarinat* (*The Tales of Ensign Stål*) that catapulted him to fame as a national poet. The ballad series was about Finland's war of 1808–09 and the bravery of the Finnish soldiers fighting alongside Swedish troops. The first of these ballads was *Our Land*, which was later adopted as Finland's national anthem, with music by Pacius.

Aleksis Kivi (1834–72) wrote the first novel in Finnish, entitled *Seven Brothers*. The stubbornness, endurance, and love of liberty of the brothers of the story continue to elicit the admiration of Finns today. Minna Canth (1844–97) was Finland's first major playwright. Her works, drawing on her experience as a wife and widow, were an inspiration to the workers' and women's movements. The best-known novel in Finland is *The Unknown Soldier* by Väinö Linna. A powerful anti-war statement, it is a realistic portrayal of war from the point of view of an ordinary soldier.

The works of J.L. Runeberg were written in Swedish and translated into Finnish.

MUSIC

Traditional folk music dominated the Finnish music scene until the 19th century, when composers began to draw inspiration from other sources. Since then, many performers and composers have established a reputation for themselves abroad.

The first notable name in Finnish music was Fredrik Pacius, who composed the score for *Our Land*. He also set up the first orchestra and choir in Helsinki.

Half of Finland's writers and poets are women.

Finnish opera singers have also met with success on the international stage. Soprano Aino Ackté set the pace in the early 1900s. She founded the Savonlinna Opera Festival, which helped to nurture future opera talents. Other famous names in opera include mezzo-soprano Monica Groop, soprano Karita Mattila, and Matti Salminen, whose rich bass voice has been likened to that of the legendary Finnish opera singer Martti Talvela (1935–89). All of these contemporary opera singers have performed in the world's great opera houses.

The Finns are fond of light music by dance bands and, for many years, Toivo Kärki reigned as the most popular composer and Dallapé, the best dance band. Finland has also made a mark internationally in the world of popular music with hits from groups such as Trio Töykeät (jazz), HIM (rock), Nightwish (metal), Värttinä (folk), and electronic dance DJ (disc-jockey) Ville Virtanen, better known as Darude.

The Finns take their music seriously as it is considered a way of preserving their cultural heritage. Music is offered as a subject in some schools in Finland while as many as 50,000 students take up lessons in 150 private music institutes. There are 30 professional orchestras in the country, more per capita than anywhere else in the world.

Many Finnish musicians, composers, and conductors have made a name for themselves, not only at home, but also abroad. Some of them are very young, such as Mikko Franck, who started conducting professionally in 1997, when he was only 17. In 2003, before turning 23, he made his conducting debut on the international stage, leading orchestras in Berlin, London, Israel, and Munich. In 2004 he was appointed the music director for the Finnish National Opera.

Folk musicians in Helsinki.

Other famous conductors include Esa-Pekka Salonen, Osmo Vänskä, and Jukka-Pekka Saraste.

JEAN SIBELIUS

Jean Sibelius is Finland's best-known composer. His name is equated with Finnish music throughout the world. *Finlandia*, for which Sibelius drew inspiration from the local landscape, became an anthem of the Finnish independence movement. For many years, the Russians refused to allow it to be performed because of the immense national pride it expressed.

Sibelius may have been Finnish, but he was also part of a greater European musical tradition. He traveled to Munich and Bayreuth in Germany in 1894 and was influenced by Tchaikovsky and German symphonic composers like Wagner and Beethoven. His *First Symphony*, first performed in 1899, signalled a moving away from his national heritage. In his later compositions, particularly the *Sixth Symphony* (1923) and *Seventh Symphony* (1924), Sibelius came into his own as a composer, unbridled by time or place, and gained international recognition as a composer. His symphonies, *Finlandia*, and a composition called the *Karelia Suite* (1893), are played by orchestras all over the world, creating an awareness of Finland in the international music scene.

National composer Jean Sibelius with two of his daughters.

DANCE

Folk dances are still very much a part of the cultural landscape, but these days they are performed mainly at special events and outdoor festivals.

Dancers perform a modern ballet.

The modern dance movement, on the other hand, is gaining popularity. It began in 1922, when the Finnish National Ballet was set up as part of the Finnish National Opera. The company presented *Swan Lake* in the Russian classical ballet tradition on its opening night.

While Margaretha von Bahr is considered the doyenne of Finnish dancers, it is Jorma Uotinen who is credited with revolutionizing Finnish dance. Uotinen is Finland's best-known choreographer, performer, and proponent of experimental dance. During his tenure as artistic director for the Finland National Ballet from 1992 to 2001 he introduced a challenging repertoire that included his dynamic interpretations of classical ballet as well as contemporary dance. He is now the artistic director of the annual Kuopio Dance and Music Festival. Under his guidance, the festival has gained an international reputation, which further enhances the status of Finnish dance.

Although classical dance is highly appreciated by Finnish audiences, there is one form of dance that is much loved in the country—tango. In Finland specially-composed tango music has helped keep this dance alive over the years. Today there are many Finnish nightspots offering tango dancing. An annual Tango Festival at Seinäjoki in Southern Ostrobothnia lures thousands of visitors, and a Tango King and Tango Queen are crowned every year.

CINEMA

The Finnish film industry started in 1906 and the first talking movie was made in 1931. An average of 15 Finnish feature films are produced each year. One of the classic Finnish films is Edvin Laine's 1955 film *Tuntematon*

Sotilas (*The Unknown Soldier*), an adaptation of Väinö Linna's novel of the same name.

Aki and Mika Kaurismäki led a wave of revival in Finnish film beginning in the 1980s. Mika Kaurismäki's films often have a touch of black humor. Among his films are *The Clan* (1980), a crime story; *Cha Cha Cha* (1989), a comedy; and *Amazon* (1990), an adventure film. Mika now spends more time making films in the United States, such as *L.A. Without a Map* (1998), than in Finland. Aki Kaurismäki, his younger brother, has built up a following as a cult director. Noted for his working class trilogy, *Shadows in Paradise* (1986), *Ariel* (1988), and *The Match Factory Girl* (1990), he has also gone international, directing films in Paris, such as *Leningrad Cowboys Go America* (1989) and *La Vie Bohème* (1992). Aki Kaurismäki put Finnish filmmaking on the map when his film, *The Man Without a Past*, won the Grand Prix du Jury at the Cannes Film Festival in 2002. The movie was also nominated for an Academy Award in the Best Foreign Language Film category in 2003.

A joyful folk dance performed in traditional Finnish costume.

THEATER

Theater in Finland began with the practice of ancient folk rituals associated with hunting and fishing. These pagan customs died out with the arrival of Christianity, which then developed its own theatrical arts.

A theater performance in Savonlinna, where an opera festival is held every summer at Olavinlinna Castle.

Although the earliest drama performance in Finland was held in Turku in the 1650s, it was not until the 19th century that the country's first theaters were built. The first Finnish play, *Silmänkääntäjät* (*The Conjurers*) by Pietari Hannikainen, was performed in 1847, but it was only in 1869, when Aleksis Kivi's *Lea* was staged, that Finnish-language theater really took off. Finland has around 60 professional theatrical troupes and many amateur and youth groups.

The main theatrical cities are Helsinki, Turku, and Tampere, although there are cultural institutes in many other areas. Theater enjoys adequate state funding as it is seen as an important part of national culture. The support of the media in publicizing theater activities, the existence of numerous festivals as a platform for showcasing theater, and an inherent love for the theater among Finns have all contributed to its healthy growth.

ARCHITECTURE

Some of the older buildings in Finland reflect the country's early Swedish and Russian influences. The Finnish style can be seen in its medieval stone castles, churches, and the detailed carvings of its 18th century wooden churches and bell towers. Carl Ludvig Engel (1778–1840), who designed the neoclassical center of Helsinki, is the best-known name in 19th century Finnish architecture.

The Romantic architectural style at the beginning of the 20th century was a blend of Karelian wooden architecture, medieval stonework, and Art Nouveau style. The 1920s saw the development of a more restrained interpretation of classical architecture, followed by more functional designs as characterized by the works of Alvar Aalto (1898–1976), the father of modern Finnish architecture. Aalto has been influential in regional and urban planning, and the design of homes, churches, and larger buildings, as well as interior decoration and industrial art. His last important work was Finlandia Hall in Helsinki, a monumental concert and conference center in white marble. He considered the forest to be Finland's most important resource and continually created links back to the forest. Aalto's wife, Aino Marsio Aalto (1898–1949), is seen today as an important contributor to Aalto's work. She served as his social conscience and followed through after Aalto made the initial sketches.

A particularly well-known Finnish architect is Eliel Saarinen (1873–1950). He designed the Chicago Tribune Building, which set the standard for early skyscrapers in the United States. His son Eero Saarinen (1909–61) is known for his design of the TWA terminal at Kennedy Airport in New York City. The terminal looks like a giant prehistoric bird poised to take off in flight.

The public library in Tampere was designed by Raili and Raimo Pietilä in the form of a grouse, a bird commonly found in the Finnish countryside.

Mother of Lemminkainen by the River of Tuonela, a 1862 oil painting by Robert Wilhelm Ekman based on the *Kalevala*.

Raili Pietilä (1923–) has worked with her husband, Raimo Pietilä (1923–), on many projects, including churches, town centers, and the presidential residence. Their design style has been described by many as unconventional.

A high point of Finnish architecture can be seen in the new town of Tapiola. Created in the late 1950s, Tapiola brought together the talents of the most important Finnish architects and urbanists of the time, including Alvar Aalto, Aarne Ervi, Pauli Blomstedt, and Raili and Raimo Pietilä.

Today, the emphasis of Finnish architecture lies in creating a more human touch and harmony with the environment. The restoration and conservation of old buildings are areas of particular interest.

PAINTING AND SCULPTURE

The earliest examples of art in Finland are the Stone Age carvings on rocks left by Arctic hunters and the frescoes in the country's medieval stone churches.

Finnish art as we know it today began with the founding of the Fine Arts Society of Finland in 1848. The greatest strides were made in the 1890s when interest in the *Kalevala* and Finnish folk poetry was revived, and many artists turned to nature and Karelia as the origin of their cultural past. This gave rise to a movement known as Karelianism, which had themes centered around landscapes and fauna. It led to the flourishing of a period that was acknowledged as the golden age of Finnish art, around the end of the 19th century. The famous names of this era include history painter Albert Edelfelt, Akseli Gallen-Kallela, Eero Järnefelt, Pekka Halonen, and Juha Rissanen.

In sculpture, Wäinö Aaltonen's portrayal of Paavo Nurmi, the Olympic runner, is internationally known. Eila Hiltunen created the Sibelius Monument, which recalls the shape of organ pipes. Located in Helsinki, it is the first completely abstract monument dedicated to a person. In response to criticism, Ms. Hiltunen later added a representation of the composer's face.

DESIGN

The Finns are masters of design, gathering their inspiration from nature. The curving shores of Finnish lakes, for instance, are said to have influenced the works of many artists, such as Alvar Aalto's celebrated Savoy vase.

Finnish textiles and rugs reflect the colors of changing seasons, while glass designers adopt many motifs from flora and fauna. Wood remains the most popular material for designers working by hand.

Finnish design was taught as early as the 19th century and made its international launch at the Paris World Exhibition in 1900. It has a classic quality about it. Its clean, modern lines have an element of timelessness. The designs are also practical, as reflected in Marimekko's popular textiles for household use, the enamel kitchenware of Heikki Orvola, and the household articles of Timo Sarpaneva. Tapio Wirkkala, a glass designer known for his iceberg designs, Kaj Franck, known for his textures, ceramics, and glass, and Timo Sarpaneva, known for his graphic design and also ceramics and glass creations, have all acquired international reputations.

The artistic designs found in glass and silver objects are good buys for tourists hunting for Finnish products to take home as souvenirs. Equally avant garde in design and style are jewelry and furniture. Many Finnish designers also create designs for industry, and the lines between art and design are constantly being blurred.

"This nation faces any storm like mountain rock. Its joy is in tranquility, but in its travail it would be content to eat of hunger's bread while spurning alien grain."

—Finnish poet Eino Leino

LEISURE

THE FINNS LOVE the outdoors, which is not surprising considering how much open space they have. For hundreds of years, they have developed their physical strength, endurance, and speed through their love of the outdoors, and have built up a strong reputation of producing long-distance runners who perform well in marathons.

From as early as 1640, the Royal Academy of Turku had a swordsmanship instructor. Sports were incorporated into military life back in the 1780s and the army has, to this day, relied on long-distance cross-country skiing as a means of developing the endurance of its conscripts.

Above: **People playing chess in Hesperian Park in Helsinki.**

Opposite: **A group of cycling enthusiasts in Helsinki.**

Even preschool children participate in sports and often continue enjoying sports till they are senior citizens. Winter sports, especially cross-country skiing, are popular. Mass skiing events each weekend during the winter season help to fuel enthusiasm for the sport. The biggest annual event is the 47-mile (75-km) Finlandia Skiing Marathon from Hämeenlinna to Lahti, which attracts well over 10,000 participants. When the snow season is over, the traveler can often spot Finns out on the road, looking as if they were skating on shortened skis. They are actually training for long-distance skiing using special mini-skis fitted with wheels.

Swimming also has a strong following and, thanks to heated indoor pools, the sport can be enjoyed even during the winter season. Other popular sports include cycling, jogging, soccer, and *pesäpallo* (PAY-sa-PAHL-lo), a sort of baseball. Although soccer is popular, the Finns are nowhere near the top of the European league. American football is also played and the Finns have become the European champions in the game. There are also ample opportunities for fishing and boating, as so much of the country is covered by water.

The sports that draw the largest number of spectators are soccer, ice hockey, track and field events, and skiing. There is probably a club for every kind of sport in Finland, with several clubs spread throughout the country for the more popular sports.

HIKING

Finland's vast areas of wilderness make it a wonderful place for hiking. In the fall, Finns often go for walks in the forest to gather mushrooms and pick wild berries. A network of well-marked trails and closely-spaced footpaths makes hiking easy, even for someone unfamiliar with the Finnish forest. The Finns have a choice of 29 nature reserves to hike in. These have wilderness huts and camping facilities for overnight hikers.

ORIENTEERING

Another sport that is suited to Finland's natural rugged terrain is orienteering, and it has a large following among young and old alike. Navigational and map-reading skills are important to successful orienteering. Essentially, it involves cross-country running where an orienteer completes a route, detailed with landmarks. Using a map and a compass, the orienteer has to move from one landmark to another until he reaches the finish line. There are orienteering clubs all over Finland and orienteers take to the countryside on weekends to enjoy their sport.

The Finnish countryside beckons hikers with its lakes, hills, and wooded terrain.

106

A Finnish name that is synonymous with orienteering worldwide is Suunto, maker of compasses and precision instruments.

WATER SPORTS AND FISHING

With a total coastline of more than 25,000 miles (40,000 km), which includes the mainland and thousands of islands, boating is big business in Finland. In summer, canoeists take to the lakes, rivers, and even the seas around the skerries and islets of the Åland archipelago. Out in the open sea and along the coastline, the sails of yachts and dinghies dot the horizon. The waters around the Åland Islands are also popular sailing grounds. The boating season is from late-May to late-September.

Finland's thousands of lakes offer many opportunities for fishing. The best time for fishing is in spring and fall.

The Finns enjoy angling for fish when they are picnicking by a stream or lake and will pan-fry their catch in the open air. Anglers can also fish from boats out at sea or from the coastline. The species of fish caught are usually perch, cod, pike, whitefish, rainbow trout, sea trout, and Atlantic salmon. Even in winter, when the lakes freeze, the Finns fish simply by making a hole in the ice!

HUNTING

Hunting for moose, hare, deer, and birds like black grouse and capercaillie is another favorite pastime. Each year, as many as 40,000 licenses for hunting elk are issued. Permits are also required from landowners, and these are usually handled by hunting associations, of which there are 3,500 in Finland.

Elk hunting is still a popular pastime in the countryside, where the meat of elk is traditional local fare.

The hunting season starts at the end of August. The participants are usually men and a strong sense of camaraderie develops as they share the tasks of camping, picnicking, stalking prey in the woods or out on lakes in boats, or with a dog if they are hunting birds. Hunting has also become a big earner for tourism, especially in the north. Every year, sportsmen from Central Europe travel to Finland to partake in the unique wilderness experience found in the vast wild landscape of Lapland.

A reindeer in deep snow. There are several different types of game in Finland, but hunting is well-regulated with the imposition of strictly-managed quotas during the hunting season.

HARNESS RACING

An unusual sport is harness racing, a spin-off from horse riding, which is also popular. Also called trotting, harness racing is a big spectator sport where horses compete against each other pulling two-wheeled carts. About 700 races are held annually. The biggest race track in Finland is Vermo, just outside Helsinki, which ranks among the largest in Europe. About 80 races are held there every year, usually on Wednesdays and Sundays.

SHOOTING RAPIDS

Shooting rapids on large rubber rafts is a popular pastime enjoyed by both young and old on a number of rivers. The fun comes from riding over swift-flowing rapids in inflatable rafts, hence, the alternative name of whitewater rafting for this sport. Operators of this activity provide the necessary equipment of life jacket, waterproof trousers, and rubber boots.

THE OLYMPICS

Finland's first entry into the Olympics was in 1906 at the intermediate games held in Athens. It marked its participation with a victory in wrestling by Verner Weckman. In 1912, Finland won nine gold medals at the Stockholm Olympics; three were won by long-distance runner Hannes Kolehmainen, who achieved victory in the 5,000-meter and 10,000-meter events, and in the marathon. From 1906 to 1988, Finland won 133 Olympic gold medals, of which 32 were earned in the Winter Games.

The Finns are especially strong in the long-distance running and javelin events. Two runners in particular have made a name for themselves—Paavo Nurmi and Ville Ritola. Nurmi is the most famous Finnish athlete of all time. He won nine gold and three silver medals in the Olympics between 1920 and 1928. Ritola won five golds. In the 1970s the top name in running was Lasse Virén, who won the 5,000-meter and 10,000-meter events in the 1972 and 1976 Olympics.

In javelin, Finland scored sensational victories, particularly in the Olympics between 1908 and 1936. Even in modern times, Finnish javelin throwers continue to shine. In the 1988 Seoul Olympics, for instance, the Finns won the gold and bronze medals. In the 1992 Barcelona Olympics, the country walked away with a silver.

The Finns have also made a mark in other sports, such as canoeing. Top oarsman Perti Karpinnen, who was Finland's Sportsman of the Year in 1979 and 1980, and Mikko Kolehmainen, who won a gold in the 1992 Barcelona Games for canoeing, have boosted the popularity of the sport.

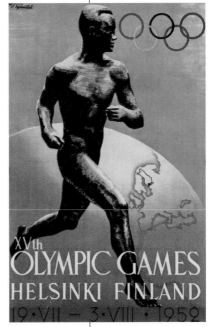

A poster publicizes the Olympic Games held in Helsinki in 1952.

Helsinki was host of the Olympic Summer Games in 1952.

Above: **Finland's Marko Yli-Hannuksela celebrates his triumph in the 74 kg category qualifying match for the men's Greco-Roman wrestling event at the Athens 2004 Olympic Games.**

Opposite: **Cross-country skiing in Finland.**

The Finns are also top contenders in winter sports, winning numerous gold medals in cross-country skiing in the Olympic winter games and world championships. Ski champions in the past included Veli Saarinen, Veikko Hakulinen, and Eero Mäntyranta among the men, and Helena Takalo and Hikka Riihivuori for the women.

Marja-Liisa Kirvesniemi was the darling of the nation when she won three gold medals and one bronze for cross-country skiing in the 1984 Sarajevo Winter Olympics. Her husband, Harri Kirvesniemi, is also a champion skier in his own right, having won medals in the Olympics and world championships. The latest skiing star is Marjo Matikainen, who won a gold and two bronze medals in the 1988 Calgary Winter Olympics.

The Finns are equally strong in ski jumping. The most famous Finnish ski jumper is world master and Olympic champion Matti Nykänen, who was unsurpassed in this event in the 1980s. In the Calgary Winter Olympics, he became the first ski jumper ever to win three golds in the same games. A ski jump is named after him in his hometown of Jyväskylä.

Toni Nieminen made a name for himself when he became the youngest winner ever in the history of the Winter Olympics. At 17 years of age, he won two gold medals and one bronze for skiing in the 1992 Olympics in Albertville, Canada. Nieminen also won a gold medal in the 1992 ski jumping World Cup.

Ice hockey is just as popular, with junior leagues formed for promising youngsters. Finnish players, like Jarri Kurri, have done so well that they have moved to the United States to join professional teams.

One of the country's top winter sportsmen is Janne Lahtela, who grabbed the gold in the men's moguls free-style skiing event in the 2002 Winter Olympics held in Salt Lake City, Utah. Before that, he won a silver for the men's free-style skiing event at Nagano in 1998. In the 2002 Olympics, Finland also won a team gold medal for the Nordic combined event, which involves competing in cross-country skiing and ski jumping.

In the 2006 Winter Olympics in Turin, a silver medal went to Tanja Pontiainen for the women's alpine skiing event while her compatriot, 25-year-old Matti Hautamäki, fondly called "The Flying Young Finn," won a silver medal for ski jumping. He won a bronze for the same event in the 2002 Winter Olympics.

Markku Uusipaavalniemi, the country's top curler, brought home the silver medal for men's curling, a sport involving two teams sliding stones into a target circle, at the 2006 Olympics. Before that, in 2000, he led Finland's national curling team to victory at the European Curling Championship.

MOTOR SPORTS

The Finns shine in motor racing. Well-known names who have won many world events include Markku Alen, Ari Vatanen, Timo Salenen, Juha Kankkunen, and Hannu Mikkola.

Pekka Vehkonen dominates motorcross racing, while Keke Rosberg achieved renown when he became Finland's first Formula One driver and the first Finn to win the world championship in 1982.

"We Finns have never been brilliant team players. But we shine in those sports that demand courage and the ability to make independent decisions. That's how Lasse Virén, Paavo Nurmi, and many others have succeeded in grueling long-distance running. That's also the way that we struggle by ourselves in rallies against the clock. Finns don't want to lose!"

—Rally driver Markku Alen

111

A statue of long-distance runner Paavo Nurmi stands outside the Olympic Stadium in Helsinki. The famous Paavo was said to have "run Finland onto the map of the world."

The most famous name in recent times is Mika Häkkinen, nicknamed "The Flying Finn." He was a member of the famous McLaren team, which is rated among the top teams in Formula One racing. Häkkinen competed for 11 seasons in the world's top motor racing event, the Formula One, winning 20 races and two world championships in 1998 and 1999. For years, he was the only real competition for German-born Michael Schumacher, holder of seven World Drivers' Championships since 1994. Häkkinen retired in 2001, handing over the wheel to his compatriot Kimi Räikkönen, another McLaren team member.

SUPPORT FOR SPORTS

Finland has several sports associations that are umbrella organizations for sports clubs. The biggest association is Suomen Valtakunnan Urheiluliitto (SU-OH-men VAHL-tah-KOON-nahn OOR-hey-loo-LEE-to), also known as the Finnish Central Sports Federation. The associations usually award training grants to their members who are top athletes. Olympic participants are given funds by the Finnish Olympic Committee.

There are specialized sports institutes in the country as well as centers of research and instruction. The major centers are the University of Jyväskylä, the University of Tampere, and the UKK Institute (named after President Urho Kekkonen), also in Tampere. Funding for sports comes from the state-owned Veikkaus (VAYK-hows), which operates football pools, trotting races, the national lottery, and other smaller lotteries.

Winners in international competitions are usually given a hero's welcome and receive rewards, such as houses that are financed by

THE FINNISH SAUNA

If there is one single item that is quintessentially Finnish, it is the sauna. The sauna was traditionally used as a kind of bathhouse. When people lived in forests, they had a log cabin where they could keep a fire going to keep warm, relax, and wash themselves. Babies were also born in the sauna, as it was warm. And when houses had no shower or bathrooms, a weekly visit to the sauna was the only way to keep clean.

Today the sauna has endured. Even though modern homes are equipped with modern bathrooms, it is still a tradition for families and friends to get together in the sauna to relax. It has become a social ritual.

Many homes have private saunas and there is a sauna in every apartment complex. Families with second homes by the lake and those living in rural areas have a separate log cabin housing the sauna, where they gather on Saturday evenings to relax. The sauna tradition is well-suited to Finland's forests, which are the source of the sauna's building materials and fuel. The traditional smoke sauna, which has no chimney, is preferred, as the heat is said to be gentler. It takes seven hours to bring the sauna to the right temperature, and all smoke is expelled before anyone goes in. It is a tradition to jump into the lake to cool off between visits to the sauna, or to roll in the snow if it is winter.

The Finns also use birch leaves to clean themselves in their sauna—it has the same effect as soap—and they hit each other with *vihta* (VEE-ta) twigs to stimulate blood circulation and "beat out" tiredness from the body. After the cleansing ritual, the Finns indulge in a "sauna supper." Any Finn who invites a guest to take a sauna prepares a meal or at least coffee. While in the sauna, much salt is lost from the body due to perspiration, so salted dishes are usually served during the meal. These may include salted herring eaten with hot boiled potatoes, anchovies, smoked fish, sardines, or a salad of salted mushrooms.

Most Finnish urban homes even have their own saunas. These are small, high-tech, electric-operated saunas that heat up in a matter of minutes.

generous donors. Finland's interest in sports is demonstrated by the number of world-sporting events it has hosted. These include the 1952 Olympic Games and the first World Athletics Championships in 1983, both of which were held in Helsinki, as well as several world ice hockey and skiing championships.

FESTIVALS

FINNISH FESTIVALS HAVE PAGAN roots and in ancient times, when farming was the main activity, were linked to the seasons. The traditional relationship of the Finns to nature can be traced to the time when they worshipped many gods and spirits that symbolized nature and the elements. The most important god of all was Ukko (OO-ko), the god of thunder and lightning, and his wife Rauni (RA-ow-nay), Mother Nature, both of whom were believed to take care of weather and the seasons. Ukko gave the Finns their word for thunder: *ukkonen* (OO-ko-nen).

Christianity came to Finland at the end of 1000 A.D. but could not wipe out the old beliefs that were part of everyday life; the Finns simply transposed ancient rituals linked to nature into celebrations of Christian feasts and saints. Even after the Reformation in the 16th century, when Catholicism and the saints were no longer embraced in Finland, the old legends and traditions survived.

EASTER

Easter is a Christian festival, but in Finland it is linked to ancient customs, such as the burning of bonfires to prevent witches and spirits from harming precious farm cattle. An early Catholic tradition involved burning a scarecrow-like effigy of Judas in the bonfire on Good Friday. Today, customs have changed. Young girls, disguised as witches and armed with willow twigs decorated with colored paper and feathers, go from house to house to wish people good luck and prosperity.

SHROVE TUESDAY

Laskiainen (LAS-kee-eye-nen), also known as Shrove Tuesday, is celebrated seven weeks before Easter. It is a time for merrymaking as it signals the

Above: **Easter decorations include chicks, eggs, pussy willow, and a straw doll. In Finland, the occasion is a curious blend of religious and pagan practices.**

Opposite: **A Finnish girl with a medieval wreath of flowers on her head.**

Finnish women dress up in medieval clothes for a rural festival.

Folk traditions and customs from Sweden, Russia, and Germany exist alongside Christian beliefs to create the many holidays and celebrations observed in a year.

end of the annual work cycle and is just before Lent, when people are expected to be somber in their behavior.

SLEEPYHEAD DAY

According to Finnish custom, anyone sleeping late on this day will feel tired for the rest of the year. The Finns call the day Unikeonpäivä (OO-nee-KAY-on-pai-va) and it falls on July 27. It commemorates the ancient legend of the seven martyrs of Ephesus who fled from the tyrannical Roman Emperor Decius in A.D. 249 and slept in a cave until A.D. 447. Sleepyhead Day is celebrated in places like Naantali and Hanko.

CHRISTMAS

The greatest rejoicing occurs during Christmas, the most important event of the Finnish festive calendar. Known as Joulu (YO-lo), it coincides with the darkest day of the year (December 23), which signaled, in ancient times, the end of the harvest. It was thus an occasion for feasting. It also marked the beginning of winter for which food was collected and stored to last the long cold season. There was reason to rejoice before the hardship began.

The Christmas tree was only introduced in the last century but has become an integral part of the Finnish Christmas. Originally, Father Christmas appeared in the form of a goat and threw presents into the doorways of houses. The appearance of a goat stemmed from pagan days when the worship of Thor, the Swedish god of thunder, included the worship of his goat. In the past, someone carrying a goat's head would burst into the parties of merrymakers. After nightlong celebrations of singing and dancing, the goat would "die" and then return to life.

In 1927 a children's radio program introduced the modern Father Christmas who brought gifts to children from his home in Lapland in his reindeer-drawn sleigh. The notion stuck. Today, children the world over are enticed to spend winter holidays in Lapland with Santa Claus. His "home" is decked with all kinds of Christmas-related items and he answers letters sent by those unable to visit him in person.

SAINT STEPHEN'S DAY

Known as Tapaninpäivä (TAH-pa-neen-PAI-va), December 26 was a day when people would ride in sleighs drawn by foals harnessed for the first time, an event to commemorate Saint Stephen, the patron saint of horses. As such, Boxing Day is also known as Saint Stephen's Day.

Santa Claus has a workshop in Lapland near Rovaniemi, and there is a special post office that replies to cards and letters received from all over the world.

THE MIDSUMMER BONFIRE

Midsummer is a festival of light, celebrating the summer solstice, when the day is at its longest. The celebration usually takes place on Midsummer Eve, also known as the eve of the Feast of Saint John the Baptist, on June 23.

Known as Juhannus (YOO-hahn-oos) in Finland, the celebration is said to be Christian in origin. It was believed that the doors of the underworld were open on this day, letting out spirits and ghosts to roam the streets and infest the air. Thousands of bonfires are lit in the belief that, by burning a bonfire, the air will be purified so that the spirits can do no harm.

Others believe that the event is more likely a folk tradition associated with this magical nightless day. That it is the day of the most light is reason enough for merrymaking. It was also a celebration associated with growth, life, and fertility.

Cattle were decorated with garlands of flowers, while young maidens would sleep with a sprig of nine herbs under their pillows, so that they would dream of their future bridegrooms. If girls looked into a pool of water, it was said that they could see the face of their sweetheart. Many of these customs are still practiced today as a source of amusement.

Other customs date back to pre-Christian times, when magic was used to promote a bountiful harvest and fertility in the coming year. Houses, boats, and buses are covered with fresh birch branches. In many places in Finland, doorways continue to be adorned with young birch trees, while those living on the Swedish-speaking Åland Islands put up Midsummer poles. These poles, erected in the midst of a bonfire pile, are decorated

Midsummer bonfires lend an air of festivity. In Finland, weddings at Midsummer are quite popular.

with wooden ships and boats, and people dance around them. Midsummer supper tables are decorated with birch and flowers.

Midsummer bonfires are lit throughout Finland. Families and friends gather at lakeside cottages to make their own bonfires, dancing around them and singing traditional songs. They stay up all night celebrating. The biggest bonfire in Helsinki is at the Seurasaari open-air folk museum, where cultural dances are also held as part of the festivities.

NAME DAY

The Finns celebrate two birthdays a year! One is the day when they were born and the other is the day of their name. The Finnish calendar is filled with days that have one or more names associated with them and the day bearing one's name is considered one's Name Day. The tradition evolved from saints' days observed in the past by Finns as members of the Roman Catholic Church.

It is customary for friends and relatives to wish one "Happy Name Day" and to give the person flowers and presents on his or her Name Day. The occasion is also celebrated with a birthday cake and candles.

Ruut (Ruth) Rotko, who celebrates her name day on January 4 and her birthday on May 27, says, "People always know your Name Day but not necessarily your birthday."

INDEPENDENCE DAY

Finland's Independence Day, on December 6, is one of the country's most important dates. If the weather pattern is normal, there is likely to be a fresh blanket of snow to enhance the day's celebrations. Different parts of the country have their

"Widespread they stand, the Northland's dusky forests, ancient, mysterious, brooding savage dreams; within them dwells the Forest's mighty god, and wood-sprites in the gloom weave magic secrets."

—Finnish composer
Jean Sibelius

A Midsummer pole stands in the Åland Islands.

own festivities to commemorate the day in 1918 when Finland became an independent republic.

Helsinki is the most important place for celebrations, which start at 9:00 A.M. with a flag-raising ceremony. A commemorative daytime service is then held. In the afternoon, there is a procession from the Hietaniemi Graveyard to Senate Square. This solemn procession of university students is perhaps the most moving of all the commemorative ceremonies. The event is held to remember those who died helping Finland gain its independence. Lighted candles are placed on the graves to burn all evening, illuminating the dark, snowy stillness—a befitting end to the day's events.

Above: **Traditional students' torch march at Senate Square in Helsinki, held on the evening of Independence Day.**

Opposite: **A boy in traditional Sami costume performs with a drum in celebration of the New Year at a festival in northern Finland.**

MAY DAY

May Day, on May 1, is another holiday celebrated with much enthusiasm in Finland. There are parades, speeches, fairs, and concerts to mark the occasion. Factories that pride themselves on running their operations all year round are closed on two days of the year: Christmas and May Day. May 1 is also seen as a celebration of the coming of spring.

STUDENTS' DAY

This celebration begins on the evening of May Day, when students in Helsinki gather at the fountain of a mermaid near the harbor. At midnight, a student climbs the statue to place a student's cap on its head. The cap is white with a black visor. The festivities continue into the next day with processions and more merrymaking.

CALENDAR OF PUBLIC HOLIDAYS

New Year's Day	January 1
Epiphany	January 6
Good Friday	March/April
Easter	March/April
May Day	May 1
Ascension Day	May
Whitsun	May
Midsummer's Day	third weekend in June
All Saints' Day	November 1
Independence Day	December 6
Christmas Day	December 25
Boxing Day/Saint Stephen's Day	December 26

"This nation's roots are deep and firm and mountain strong. Its people love this land alone, its laws and language that they own, the ancient songs that hold and keep their fathers' mem'ries green."

—*Eino Leino*, This Nation on a Rock

NEW YEAR'S EVE

On New Year's Eve, a small piece of tin is melted, thrown into a bucket of water, and left to harden. The shape that it forms is purported to foresee the future: lumps and bulges signify money coming in, black spots are a sign of impending sadness, while a boat shape predicts an event associated with travel.

FOOD

TYPICAL FINNISH CUISINE is a blend of Russian and Swedish influences, with a bit of the Scandinavian and Baltic thrown in. It tends to change seasonally, reaping the generous bounty of Mother Nature. Indeed, the country's forests, rivers, and lakes are the richest sources of food. Geographical location also plays a part, giving rise to regional specialties.

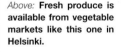

Above: **Fresh produce is available from vegetable markets like this one in Helsinki.**

Opposite: **Finnish girls in medieval costumes prepare food at a carnival.**

Recipes are passed down from one generation to another, and flavors are kept as natural as possible. Finnish food is thus rather simple, but wholesome and prepared from the freshest ingredients. Meals are eaten with rye bread on the side.

What is truly astonishing is the variety of dishes available each season. As a nation of thousands of lakes, it is not surprising that much of the local cuisine revolves around fish. During the summer, salmon, Baltic herring, and whitefish are available all over the country. Crayfish are also available from the end of July through September.

While fish, especially salmon, is enjoyed grilled or smoked, the Finns prefer to boil freshly-caught crayfish, which tastes and looks like a miniature version of the American lobster. Other times of the year, there are different species of freshwater fish, like rainbow trout, pike, Finnish whitefish, perch, grayling, and zander.

Summer also yields a great variety of vegetables and berries. A favorite vegetable dish is made of new potatoes that are freshly dug up in June. They are boiled in dill and served with butter and raw herring. A wide range of berries is used to make pastries to satisfy the Finnish sweet tooth. A visitor to the country should not miss tasting blueberry pie, wild strawberries with cream, and the many liqueurs made from berries, such as arctic brambleberries and cloudberries.

Autumn is a time for wild mushrooms, such as chanterelles and morels, which are often made into a delicious, light, and creamy soup known as *korvasienikeitto* (KORR-va-sie-ni-KAY-ee-toh). Autumn is also the hunting season for game, such as elk, hare, black grouse, capercaillie, and ptarmigan, all of which are plentiful in Finland.

In winter, body-warming soups and pies are popular, as well as turnips and rutabagas, two winter roots. Fish is also featured in soups, and *lohikeitto* (LOH-i-KAY-ee-toh), which is salmon soup with potatoes, dill, and milk, is especially tasty. A very special fish dish appearing on restaurant menus in February is *mäti* (MA-tee), a roe from freshwater fish, dubbed Finnish caviar. Yellow or orange in color, the fine roe is

Sorbet with cloudberries and strawberries, a typical Finnish dessert that makes good use of the plentiful supply of fresh fruits available in the country.

exquisite when served with chopped onions and *smetana* (SMAY-ta-na), or sour cream.

Oddly enough, it is not always easy to find typical Finnish food outside private homes. Helsinki, for instance, has many excellent Russian restaurants, while menus in most restaurants tend to be international. Meat dishes, for instance, are cooked French-style, unless it is game or reindeer. However, fish, soups, and desserts are usually in the Finnish tradition.

An alternative to eating out in a restaurant would be to visit one of the many small and cozy outdoor cafes for a light meal. Most people drop by to have coffee with pastries or the quintessential Finnish *pulla* (POO-lah), a sweet bread with cardamom that is sprinkled with sugar.

SMORGASBORD

Smorgasbord is not Finnish in origin, as it was the Swedes who made it famous. Still, a foreigner staying in a hotel in Finland will often come across smorgasbord served for breakfast or lunch. It includes a wide array of dishes ranging from smoked salmon and salami to reindeer meat, cheeses, and salads. Smorgasbord is an excellent way to sample a variety of Finnish dishes.

A smorgasbord offering a variety of salads and Finnish food.

CHRISTMAS FARE

Christmas is a time for feasting. The celebration begins on December 24 and starts with breakfast, when a traditional rice pudding is eaten. An almond is hidden in the pudding, and whoever bites into it has to "pay" a penalty such as singing a song or reciting a poem. Then follows the

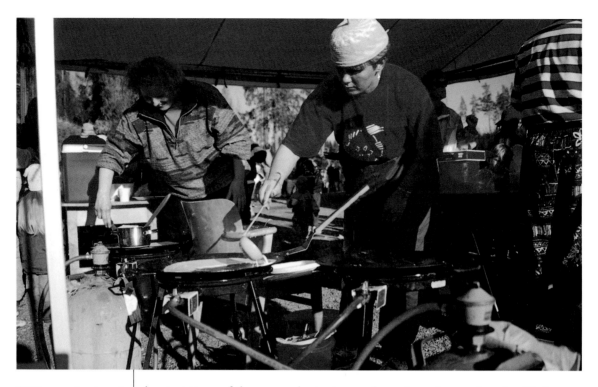

Making pancakes for out-door festivities.

busiest time of the year—last minute shopping, decorating the Christmas tree, and wrapping the presents.

In the early evening, many people go to the cemetery to spare a moment of thought for their departed ones. They pray and light candles on family graves. Then, it is time to enjoy a sauna before sitting down to feast.

A glass of warming grogg or spiced mulled wine is first served as an aperitif to get the party going. The meal itself begins with lightly-salted salmon, herring prepared in various ways, and other types of cold hors d'oeuvres. The main dish is glazed ham cooked overnight in a slow oven. It is accompanied by other oven-baked dishes made from carrots, potatoes, rutabagas, and liver, and slices of a Christmas bread that is sweet and spicy. A home-brewed ale is traditionally drunk at Christmas. Dessert may be prune parfait or pies made from berries. The rest of the evening is spent at home, chatting and drinking in front of a fire.

Those who choose to enjoy a sauna at this time usually follow it with a meal of fish, ham, and rice pudding. In both the city and countryside, animals and birds are given extra food.

Christmas Day starts early when Finnish families go to church. Then, it is time for more feasting on rich Christmas pies such as *joulutorttu* (YO-loo-TORR-too) or tiny delectable pastries stuffed with pulped prunes, gingerbread, date, and fruitcake. Boxing Day on December 26 is reserved for visiting friends and relatives and finishing the Christmas food. A dance in the evening usually marks the end of the festive season.

REGIONAL SPECIALTIES

Karelia in the east and Lapland in the north boast the greatest variety of regional specialties in Finland. *Karjalanpaisti* (KAR-yah-lahn-PA-I-stee) is a Karelian meat casserole, a hearty blend of beef, pork, and mutton, eaten traditionally in winter.

Karjalanpiirakat (KAR-yah-lahn-PEE-rah-kaht) are Karelian pastries made of rye dough that are filled with rice or mashed potatoes and served hot with hard-boiled eggs and butter. Also from eastern Finland, particularly Kuopio, is *kalakukko* (KAH-lah-KOO-ko), which is fish and bacon baked inside a crust of rye bread.

A Sami man cooking over an open fire.

Eating reindeer is typically Finnish and reindeer meat can be prepared in various ways and eaten in many forms, grilled as steaks or chops, or cooked in stews. In Lapland, *poronpaisti* (POH-ron-PA-I-stee), a reindeer roast, and *poronkäristys* (POh-rohn-KA-rees-toos), which are thin strips of smoked reindeer meat, are common. *Mustamakkara* (MUST-ah-MAH-ka-ra) is grilled black pudding, a Tampere specialty, served with red whortleberries.

DRINKS

The Finns enjoy drinking and have all sorts of alcoholic concoctions made with locally-available ingredients. Finland is noted for its berry liqueurs, which are fairly sweet, and its grain spirits.

Traditional local fare in Lapland. Reindeer and elk meat are still popular rural dishes.

There is *lakkalikööri* (LAK-ka-LEE-koo-ee-ree) made from golden yellow cloudberries that grow on arctic and subarctic bogs. The rich, strong-flavored liqueur is reputedly full of vitamin C.

Another strong berry liqueur is *puolukkalikööri* (POO-loo-kah-LEE-koo-ee-ree), made from red whortleberries or cowberries.

The rare arctic brambleberry, which looks like a wild strawberry, makes a sweet but delicate liqueur called *mesimarjalikööri* (MES-see-mar-ya-LEE-koo-ee-ree).

The best-known Finnish grain spirit is Finlandia vodka, which comes in a frosted bottle, as seen in most international duty-free shops. However, the connoisseurs' choice seems to be *Koskenkorva-Viina* (KOS-ken-KOR-va-VEE-na), a 38-percent vodka distilled from wheat.

The Finns have their own version of champagne—a sparkling wine fermented from white currants and gooseberries. Beer is light, similar to lager, and there are different varieties: alcohol-free or low-alcohol beers that are sold in supermarkets, and strong beer available only from the Alko liquor monopoly stores. A homemade, low-alcohol beer brewed from a mixture of water, malt, sugar, and yeast is *kotikalja* (KO-tee-CAR-lee-ya), a must on every rural buffet table.

BREAD AND COFFEE

Bread is a staple in every Finnish home. In the east, it is baked weekly. In the west, some rural households still bake their bread twice a year in enormous ovens. They string up their loaves through a hole in the middle and hang them on a pole to dry. Each day, a loaf is taken down and soaked in milk before it is consumed. In the towns, there are bakeries where fresh bread can be bought daily. Bread is usually consumed at breakfast, together with cereal, oat porridge, and sausages. Sandwiches may be eaten at other times when there is a need for a quick meal.

A Finnish baker displaying bread for sale.

The Finns are avid coffee drinkers, drinking more coffee per capita than any other people in the world. Coffee is served all day. Coffee drinking is an event that should not be rushed. One sits with a friend or business associate and sips leisurely. Sandwiches and pastries are usually served.

TROUT BAKED IN FOIL

1 trout, cleaned and scaled (salmon or whitefish may be used as a substitute)
8 tablespoons (115 g) butter
1 bunch dill
Salt
Freshly-ground white pepper
Aluminium foil

Cut a sheet of aluminium foil four inches longer than the trout. Season the fish with salt and white pepper. Stuff the dill into its stomach. Grease the foil with butter. Place fish on the foil with the rest of the butter. Cut vegetables such as asparagus and carrots may be added as well. Fold the foil tightly and bake in 425°F (220°C) oven for 25 minutes. When the fish is cooked, unwrap the foil and serve it immediately.

SUMMER BERRY TART

For the pastry
A baking dish with an 11-inch diameter
Butter to grease dish
½ pound (227 g) oven-ready shortcrust pastry
Fresh raspberries
Fresh strawberries
Fresh red currants
Fresh bilberries (if bilberries are not available, blueberries can be used as a substitute)
Confectioners' sugar for dusting

For the filling
1 cup (270 g) milk
3 egg yolks
⅓ cup (85 g) sugar
¼ tablespoon (45 g) cornstarch
¼ cup (75 g) citrus liqueur

Start by preparing the filling. Heat the milk in the saucepan. In the meantime, mix together the egg yolks, sugar, and cornstarch. When they have blended well, pour the mixture into the milk and keep stirring until just before it reaches the boiling point. When the mixture has thickened, remove the saucepan from the stove. Add liqueur to the hot mixture and let it cool.

Roll out the pastry. After greasing the baking dish, spread the pastry on it. Bake in a 350°F (180°C) oven until the pastry turns golden brown. Let it cool and remove from the baking pan.

Spread the filling over the pastry and arrange the berries on top by groups. Sprinkle with confectioners' sugar if desired and serve.

A   **B**   **C**

● Capital city
● Major town
▲ Mountain Peak

Feet	Meters
16,500	5,000
9,900	3,000
6,600	2,000
3,300	1,000
1,650	500
660	200
0	0

1

● Utsjoki

NORWAY

Haltiatunturi
(4,343 ft / 1,324 m)

Inari
● Inari
Lemmen
Ivalo

▲ *Ounastunturi*

▲ *Pallastunturi*

▲ *Yllästunturi*

LAPLAND

KARELIA

Ylläs ●
Ounas
● Sodankylä
Raudan

2

Arctic Circle

S W E D E N

● Napapiiri
Rovaniemi

R
U
S
S
I
A

Kemijoki

● Kemi

NORTHERN
OSTROBOTHNIA

Karlö
● Oulu

KAINUU

3

Oulu

Pyha

CENTRAL
OSTROBOTHNIA

Oulujärvi

● Kokkola

NORTHERN
SAVONIA

Pielinen

Vallgrund

● Vaasa

OSTROBOTHNIA

● Seinäjoki

SOUTHERN
OSTROBOTHNIA

Lapuan

Keitele

CENTRAL
FINLAND

● Kuopio

NORTH
KARELIA

● Joensuu
Pielis

Jyväskylä ●

Varkaus ●

SOUTHERN
SAVONIA

4

SATAKUNTA

Näsijärvi

PIRKANMAA

Iyväskylä ●

● Savonlinna

● Pori

● Tampere

Mikkeli ●

PÄIJÄNNE
TAVASTIA

Saimaa

● Imatra

● Rauma

TAVASTIA
PROPER

Lahti ●

SOUTH KARELIA

FINLAND
PROPER

Hämeenlinna ●

EASTERN
UUSIMAA

● Kouvola

KYMENLAAKSO

ÅLAND
ISLANDS

Turku ●

Vantaa ●

Parvoo ●

● Kotka

● Turku

UUSIMAA

Kimito

Espoo ●

● HELSINKI

Mariehamn ●

5

BALTIC SEA

Gulf of Finland

Gulf
of
Bothnia

N

ESTONIA

MAP OF FINLAND

ECONOMIC FINLAND

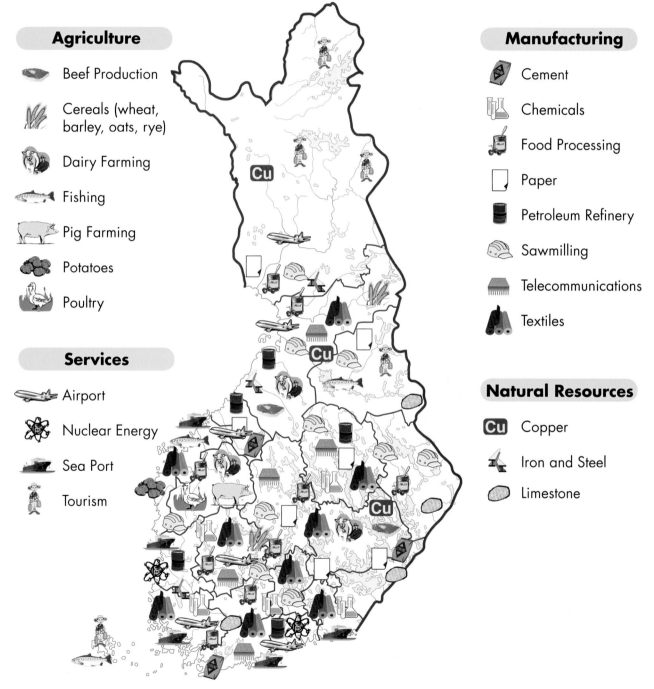

Agriculture

- Beef Production
- Cereals (wheat, barley, oats, rye)
- Dairy Farming
- Fishing
- Pig Farming
- Potatoes
- Poultry

Services

- Airport
- Nuclear Energy
- Sea Port
- Tourism

Manufacturing

- Cement
- Chemicals
- Food Processing
- Paper
- Petroleum Refinery
- Sawmilling
- Telecommunications
- Textiles

Natural Resources

- Cu Copper
- Iron and Steel
- Limestone

ABOUT THE ECONOMY

OVERVIEW
Finland began its transition from a largely-rural society to a modern industrialized nation after the end of World War II and completed it in less than half a century, experiencing quick economic growth in the process. In 1991 Finland experienced its first recession during which the economy took a nosedive and unemployment shot up. A restructuring of the economy, with emphasis given to the development of high-tech industries and telecommunications, paid off when Finland became a major exporter of cell phones and high-tech equipment in 1995. Finland has since recovered and is enjoying a buoyant economy, with unemployment at only 8.4 percent in 2005 and a per capita GDP that is on par with the United Kingdom, Germany, and France.

GROSS DOMESTIC PRODUCT (GDP)
$161.5 billion (2005)

GDP GROWTH
2.2 percent (2005)

LAND USE
Arable land 8 per cent, forest 70 per cent, others 22 per cent

CURRENCY
The euro (EUR), converted from the former markka in 2002; 1 euro = 5.95 markkas; The euro is divided into 100 cents; USD1 = 1.28 euro (November 2006)

MINERAL RESOURCES
Iron ore, copper, lead, zinc, chromite, nickel, gold, silver, limestone

AGRICULTURAL PRODUCTS
Grain (wheat, barley, oats, rye), beetroot, spinach, rutabaga, potato, cabbage, forest products, dairy farming, beef, pigs, poultry

MAJOR EXPORTS
Electronic and electrical products, pulp and paper, machinery and equipment, metal products, transportation vehicles, timber and wood, chemicals

EXPORTS OF GOODS AND SERVICES
$67.88 billion (2005)

MAJOR IMPORTS
Petroleum and petroleum products, chemicals, transportation equipment, iron and steel, machinery, foodstuffs, grain, textile yarn and fabrics

IMPORTS OF GOODS AND SERVICES
$56.45 billion (2005)

TRADE PARTNERS
Germany, Russia, Sweden, United Kingdom, United States

WORKFORCE
2.61 million (2005)

UNEMPLOYMENT RATE
8.4 percent (2005)

INFLATION RATE
1.2 percent (2005)

CULTURAL FINLAND

Ylläs
Ylläs is one of Finland's top ski centers and host to a music festival in July.

Rovaniemi
Gateway to Lapland, home of the Sami people, and the start of the Great Arctic Highway, Rovaniemi is the place to see the famous Aurora Borealis, or Northern Lights, a mysterious glow that lights up the sky on winter nights.

Kemi
It is here that one can cruise the Gulf of Bothnia on board an Arctic icebreaker for a quintessentially Finnish experience.

Pori
A music lover's haven in mid-July, when the 10-day Pori International Jazz Festival takes place, Pori offers a smorgasbord of more than 100 performances by the world's best jazz musicians.

Rauma
A UNESCO World Heritage site, Rauma's Old Town is a pedestrian's delight with its 600 wooden buildings from the 18th and 19th centuries.

Turku
Founded in the 13th century, Turku was Finland's capital until 1812 and is the seat of the country's first university. Turku is billed the country's cultural capital, and one of its top attractions is its outstanding medieval Turku Castle.

Åland
A slice of Sweden in Finland, visitors can go cruising in a wooden schooner among its 6,400 islets, enjoy traditional Midsummer festivities with maypole dancing, or visit its 14th century Kastelholm Castle.

Inari
The hub of Sami culture. Visitors can learn more about Sami culture at the open-air Siida Sami Museum, which showcases Sami history and lifestyle, and visit a reindeer farm or explore the wilderness here.

Napapiiri
This is where the Artic Circle officially begins. It is the site of the well-known Santa Claus Village, the "official" home of Santa Claus, who may be visited in his Santapark office.

Oulanka National Park
For a true wilderness experience and some of the best scenery in all of Finland, visitors may roam the fells here and stay in a wilderness hut.

Oulu
Visitors travel from different parts of the world to experience the land of the midnight sun in June and July when the sun never sets, and revel in this lively university town's outdoor bars and summer festivals.

Savonlinna
Set on two islands between two lakes, Savonlinna provides a beautiful setting for the renowned month-long Savonlinna Opera Festival in July, attracting top opera performers. The festival is held in the courtyard of Olavinlinna, the best-preserved medieval castle in Scandinavia.

Ilomantsi
Ilomantsi is Karelia at its best. It is more Russian than Finnish in culture and is the seat of the Orthodox Church.

Lappeenranta
Set on the shores of Lake Saimaa and only 18.6 miles (30 km) from the Russian border, it is the biggest inland port in Finland. Visitors may embark on the MS Karelia for a day-long cruise on the historic Saimaa Canal to Vyborg in Russia.

Helsinki
The capital of Finland since 1812, this beautiful maritime city is more cosmopolitan than truly Scandinavian, thanks to its mix of Swedish, Russian, and international influences. A cultural and high-tech hub, it is noted for its active concert scene and nightlife.

ABOUT THE CULTURE

OFFICIAL NAME
Republic of Finland
In Finnish—Suomen Tasavalta (Suomi, in abbreviated form)
In Swedish—Republiken Finland (Finland, in abbreviated form)

FLAG DESCRIPTION
The national (civil) flag of Finland is a blue rectangular Scandinavian cross on a white background. The state flag, used by the military, bears the state arms on the intersection of the cross.

TOTAL AREA
130,558 square miles (338,144 square km)

CAPITAL
Helsinki

POPULATION
5.23 million (2006 estimate)

ETHNIC GROUPS
Finn 93.4 percent, Swede 5.7 percent, Russian 0.4 percent, Estonian 0.2 percent, Roma 0.2 percent, Sami 0.1 percent

RELIGIOUS GROUPS
Lutheran National Church 84.2 percent, Orthodox Church 1.1 percent, other Christian denominations 1.1 percent, others 0.1 percent, atheist 13.5 percent

BIRTH RATE
10.45 births per 1,000 Finns (2006 estimate)

DEATH RATE
9.86 deaths per 1,000 Finns (2006 estimate)

AGE STRUCTURE
0 to 14 years: 17.1 percent (male 455,420/ female 438,719);
15 to 64 years: 66.7 percent (male 1,766,674/ female 1,724,858);
65 years and over: 16.2 percent (male 337,257/ female 508,444) (2006 estimates)

LANGUAGES
Finnish (official), Swedish (official), Sami, Russian

LITERACY RATE
For those aged 15 and above who can both read and write: 100 percent

NATIONAL HOLIDAYS
New Year's Day (January 1), Twelfth Day (January 6), Good Friday, Easter Sunday, May Day (May 1), Ascension Day, Midsummer Day (June 24), All Saints' Day (November 1), Independence Day (December 12), Christmas Day (December 25), Boxing Day (December 26)

TIME LINE

IN FINLAND	IN THE WORLD

7,500–1,500 B.C. (Stone Age)
Tribes believed to be the ancestors of the Sami arrive from eastern Europe and settle on the Arctic coast of present-day Finland. Later settlers caused the Sami to move farther north.

753 B.C.
Rome is founded.

500 B.C.– A.D. 400
The Finns, who gave the country its name, cross the Baltic to settle in Finland.

116–17 B.C.
The Roman Empire reaches its greatest extent, under Emperor Trajan (98–17).

A.D. 600
Height of the Mayan civilization

1000
The Chinese perfect gun powder and begin to use it in warfare.

1528
The Reformation reaches Finland with Mikael Agricola introducing the teachings of Martin Luther. Finland breaks away from the Catholic Church.

1530
Beginning of transatlantic slave trade organized by the Portuguese in Africa.

1550
Founding of Helsinki, or Helsingfors, by the Swedish king

1558–1603
Reign of Elizabeth I of England

1620
Pilgrims sail the *Mayflower* to America.

1714—21
The Great Wrath, the occupation of Finland by Russia, ends in 1721, with the Treaty of Uusikaupunki.

1741—43
The War of the Hats begins with Sweden attacking eastern Karelia, which is under Russian control. Russia counterattacks and occupies all of Finland in 1742, a period known as the Lesser Wrath. It ends in 1743 with the Treaty of Turku.

1776
U.S. Declaration of Independence

1789–99
The French Revolution

1809
Finland becomes an autonomous Grand Duchy of Russia. The Finns retain their own legal system and religion and are exempt from Russian military service.

1812
The Russians move the capital of Finland from Turku to Helsinki.

1861
The U.S. Civil War begins.

IN FINLAND	IN THE WORLD

1906
Finnish women are given the right to vote—the first in Europe.

1917
The Russian Revolution begins and Finland declares its independence.

1939
World War II begins. Finland declares its neutrality but is invaded by the Soviet Union. Winter War between the two countries starts.

1995
Finland becomes a member of the European Union (EU), formerly known as the European Economic Community.

1999
Finland serves as president of the EU and hosts two Head of State summits.

2000
Finland elects its first female president, Tarja Halonen, in February. On March 1, Finland's new constitution comes into force. On June 12, Helsinki celebrates its 450th anniversary of Independence. It is also named as one of nine European cities of culture for 2000.

2003
Finland elects its first female prime minister, Anneli Jäätteenmäki, in March. Two months later, she resigns. Matti Vanhanen takes over as premier.

2006
Tarja Halonen is reelected as president for a second term in January.

1869
The Suez Canal is opened.

1914
World War I begins.

1939
World War II begins.

1945
The United States drops atomic bombs on Hiroshima and Nagasaki.

1949
The North Atlantic Treaty Organization (NATO) is formed.

1991
Breakup of the Soviet Union

1997
Hong Kong is returned to China.

2001
Terrorists crash planes in New York, Washington, D.C., and Pennsylvania.

2003
War in Iraq begins.

GLOSSARY

ei (ay)
No.

eskers
Long, level ridges of sand and rock left behind when glaciers melt and recede.

Joulu (YO-lo)
The Christmas holiday.

Juhannus (YOO-hahn-oos)
Midsummer celebration held on June 23, usually highlighted by a bonfire.

kaamos (KAAH-mos)
"Sunless days" in the arctic region when the sun never rises. This season lasts nearly six months.

kantele (KAHN-tay-leh)
An ancient harplike instrument traditionally used to accompany rune singers.

kiitos (KEEH-tos)
Thank you.

kyllä (KOO-la)
Yes.

korvasienkeitto (KORR-va-sie-ni-KAY-ee-toh)
A light, creamy soup.

lohikeitto (LOH-i-KAY-ee-toh)
A salmon soup.

mäti (MA-tee)
Roe from a freshwater fish.

näkemiin (NA-kem-een)
Goodbye.

olkaa hyvä (OHL-kaah HOO-vah)
Please.

pesäpallo (PAY-sa-PAHL-lo)
A type of baseball game.

poronpaisti (POH-ron-PA-I-ees-tee)
A reindeer roast.

pulla (POO-lah)
Sweet bread flavored with cardamon and sprinkled with sugar.

saari (SAAH-ri)
Island.

smetana (SMAY-ta-na)
Sour cream.

Tapaninpäivä (TAH-pa-neen-PAI-va)
Boxing Day, on December 26.

Ukko (OO-ko)
The ancient Finnish god of thunder and lightning.

ukkonen (OO-ko-nen)
Thunder.

FURTHER INFORMATION

BOOKS

Hutchison, Linda. *Finland (Modern Nations of the World series)*. San Diego, CA: Lucent, 2004.

Lerner Publications Company Geography Department (author) and David A. Boehm (editor). *Finland—in Pictures*. Minneapolis, MN: Lerner Publications Company, 1991.

Livo, Norma J. and George Livo. *The Enchanted Wood and Other Tales from Finland*. Westport, CT: Libraries Unlimited, 1999.

Lönnrot, Elias. *The Kalevala: or Poems of the Kaleva District*. Translated by Francis Peabody Magoun, Jr. Cambridge, MA: Harvard University Press, paperback reprint edition, 2006.

Singleton, Frederick B. *A Short History of Finland*. New York: Cambridge University Press, 1990.

WEB SITES

Embassy of Finland, Washington, D.C. www.finland.org/en/

Virtual Finland. http://virtual.finland.fi/

BIBLIOGRAPHY

Charbonneau, Claudette and S.W. Meditz. *The Land and People of Finland*. New York: J.B. Lippincott, 1990.

Lerner Publications Company Geography Department (author) and David A. Boehm (editor). *Finland—in Pictures*. Minneapolis, MN: Lerner Publications Company, 1991.

Rajanen. *Of Finnish Ways*. New York: HarperCollins, 1990.

Singleton, Frederick B. *A Short History of Finland*. New York: Cambridge University Press, 1990.

Solsten, Eric and Meditz, S.W, eds. *Finland: A Country Study*. 2nd edition. Washington D.C.: U.S. Government Printing Office, 1991.

Vaananen-Jensen, Inkeri (translator). *The Fish of Gold and Other Finnish Folk Tales*. Iowa City, IA: Penfield Press, 1990.

Contemporary Art. typo.kiasma.fi/index.php?id=11&L=1&FL=0

Culture. www.kulttuuri.net/english/

Design Museum. www.designmuseum.fi/main.asp?sid=2
Festivals in Finland. www.festivals.fi/index2.php
Finnish Dance Information Center. www.danceinfo.fi/english
The Finnish Film Archive. www.sea.fi/english/
Finnish Symphony Orchestras. www.sinfoniaorkesterit.fi/engl/ehome.htm
Fiskars Village. www.fiskarsvillage.net/index_e.htm
Happenings in the capital of Finland: Helsinki.
    www.hel.fi/wps/portal/Helsinki_en/?WCM_GLOBAL_CONTEXT=/en/Helsinki/
Ministry of Education—culture. www.minedu.fi/minedu/culture/index.html
Museums. www.museoliitto.fi/suomenmuseot/english/index.html
Music Export Finland. http://musex.fi/mxf/
Virtual Finland. http://virtual.finland.fi/

INDEX